Casebook to Accompany
BUSINESS DATA COMMUNICATIONS

Casebook to Accompany
BUSINESS DATA COMMUNICATIONS

DAVID A. STAMPER
University of Northern Colorado

The Benjamin/Cummings Publishing Company, Inc.

Redwood City, California • Fort Collins, Colorado •
Menlo Park, California • Reading, Masssachusetts • New York •
Don Mills, Ontario • Wakingham, U.K. • Amsterdam • Bonn •
Sydney • Singapore • Tokyo • Madrid • San Juan

Developmental editor: Devra Lerman

ISBN: 0-8053-0304-9
ISBN: 0-8053-7722-0 (Updated Edition)

7 8 9-CRS-98 97 96 95 94 93

The Benjamin/Cummings Publishing Company, Inc.
390 Bridge Parkway
Redwood City, California 94065

CONTENTS

PREFACE

INTRODUCTION

A data communications course does not, in general, lend itself to hands-on exercises. There are several reasons for this. Some of the equipment that could be effectively used for such exercises--for example, break-out boxes, digital line monitors, and multiplexers--are not commonly found in academic departments and are rather expensive. Creating an environment for hands-on exercises may be difficult because it typically requires a variety of components--terminals, computers, cables, modems, multiplexers, software and so on. Frequently these components must be dedicated to the exercise to avoid disruption to other users. Also, designing a hands-on exercise that is meaningful without being overly complex is not easy.

An alternative to hands-on exercises is a case study. A case study allows students to apply data communications concepts to life-like situations in the absence of, or as a supplement to, hands-on exercises. Moreover, case studies do not require large investment in equipment. The five case studies and appendix in this case book are designed to augment classroom learning in data communications. Each of the cases is fictitious; however, most of the situations are based on real events or an amalgamation of real events. Actual incidents were used to promote the realism of each case.

CASE OBJECTIVES

Each of the case studies were designed to satisfy specific objectives. In some instances objectives overlap; however, where there is overlap, the intent is to give a different perspective to those objectives. For example, Case 1, The Balboa Insurance Agency and Case 5, Archer Freight Lines, both involve the use of microcomputers; however, the ways in which microcomputers are used by these companies differ significantly.

The objectives of each of the cases are summarized below.

Case 1 - The Balboa Insurance Agency. In the future, it is probable that any organization having two or more microcomputers will network those microcomputers. There are a variety of ways in which this may be accomplished. The objectives of this case is to explore the alternatives available for connecting a small number of microcomputers and the advantages and disadvantages of each alternative.

Networking microcomputers creates an environment different from that of individual workstations. This new environment requires a certain amount of centralized management. Another case objective is to explore the management and administration issues of microcomputer networks.

Case 2 - Northern State University. In all organizations, both large and small, it may happen that several networks are established. Originally, there might have been no reason or available technology to connect these networks. With today's technology, many companies with these islands of computing want to expand their data communication capabilities by interconnecting the different networks. Northern State University is one such organization. This case examines the technical and management issues of network interconnection.

Case 3 - The Associated Banks. One of the problems facing companies with distributed geographic locations is how to provide computing services to each location. The basic available approaches to this situation are centralized computing, regionalized computing, and distributed computing. This case probes these alternatives.

Case 4 - Financial Consultants International. Many of today's companies are international in scope and need an international data communications network. The complexity of implementing an international network is often considerably greater than that of implementing a national or local network. Some of these complexities arise from language differences, time zone differences, interface and power differences, and national regulations. This case examines the legal, administrative, and operations issues unique to international networks.

Case 5 - Archer Freight Lines. Microcomputers provide considerable flexibility regarding how they can be used in computer networks. In Case 1, The Balboa Insurance Agency, microcomputers were the principal source of computing power. In other networks, microcomputers are used in conjunction with larger computing systems. Archer Freight Lines is one such company. This case examines several ways in which microcomputers can be connected to a host computer. This case can also be used for network design and costing exercises.

PROBLEMS AND EXERCISES

Each case concludes with a number of problems and exercises. These are intended to emphasize the case objectives. To obtain the maximum benefit of each case, you should augment these exercises and problems. Thus, you can change or expand the case objectives and focus the case in new directions.

This case book is intended to be a supplement to the text *Business Data Communications*, Second Edition, The Benjamin/Cummings Publishing Company. All cases assume a knowledge of the related material in the text. The solution of some case exercises requires a greater level of detail than the text provides. In these instances, additional technical detail is included within the case description. Also, you may wish to consult technical manuals and periodicals to include even greater technical detail. For the most part, however, the intent is to have each of the case objectives met by the combined text and case information.

You will note that Case 4, Financial Consultants International, is considerably shorter than the other four. There are several reasons for this. First, most of the supporting information for this case is found in the associated text; therefore, the case itself consists primarily of a description of the company. Second, many aspects of international networks--for example, determining costs and establishing interfaces-- are quite complex and diverse; providing this level of minutia would make the case overly detailed and limit its effectiveness. Third, because of the aforementioned complexities, the objectives of the case are to emphasize the more manageable aspects of international networks--network configuration, network management, and network operations. If you examine this case, you will find that despite being shorter, this case is as substantial and challenging as the other four cases.

THE APPENDIX

As mentioned earlier, solution to the cases is intended to be self-contained; that is, all essential information is contained in the associated text or the case itself. To facilitate solving some of the problems relating to network costs, an appendix is provided. The appendix contains representative costs for certain network components. For consistency, the costs provided in the appendix are taken from the associated text wherever possible. You should be aware that equipment, software, and service costs are constantly changing, and you may wish to make your results more current by using current prices.

SUMMARY

Case studies provide a way to apply theory to real-life situations. The five cases in this case book represent a variety of problems being faced by many of today's companies. Investigation of these problems will promote an understanding of some of the principles of data communications design and management. In working on the case exercises, you will likely be faced with several alternatives; more than one of these alternatives may lead to a successful solution.

THE BALBOA INSURANCE AGENCY

CASE OBJECTIVES

Microcomputers have placed the power of computing in the economic range of all types of businesses. Companies, both large and small, have purchased microcomputers to solve business problems and increase personnel productivity. Often, these companies have installed several microcomputers in one location. As microcomputer technology has developed, it has become increasingly easy and cost effective to connect these systems into a network. In this case, you will evaluate the needs of a small company, the Balboa Insurance Agency, and determine how it can more effectively utilize its microcomputers. In the case exercises, you will have the opportunity to evaluate the following:

- . Various methods for configuring microcomputers to provide computing resources for a small office or work group.

- . Strengths and weaknesses for each of the configuration methods.

- . Management and administrative issues relating to sharing computer resources.

THE BALBOA INSURANCE AGENCY - AN OVERVIEW

The Balboa Insurance Agency is an insurance brokerage firm representing several different insurance companies. The agency is located in Meridian, a town with a population of approximately 60,000. Meridian is an agricultural hub city servicing the needs of its residents and a rural population of approximately 25,000. For 25 years, Balboa was owned and managed by Jack Triplett. Triplett's business philosophy was to operate from two small offices located at either end of the city for the convenience of his company's clients. Each office had four employees: two insurance broker/agents and two office administrators. Three months ago, Triplett sold his business to Barbara Holmes.

Barbara Holmes' business philosophy was different from Jack Triplett's. Although the business was successful when she bought it, she believed it would be more profitable if the two offices were consolidated. With one central office, office rental, supplies, equipment, and telephone costs can be reduced. Moreover, with one central location, the administrative staff can be reduced by one person without diminishing service. Because of the relatively small size of Meridian, the company's clients, a good number of whom live in the rural area, will not be inconvenienced to any great degree by having only one office.

With this business philosophy in mind, Holmes moved Balboa into a renovated house in the central business area. The building provides room for expansion if the company grows. Two employees left the company when it was sold--one insurance agent and one office administrator. Thus, Holmes moved into the company's new office with six employees: three insurance brokers and three office administrators.

BALBOA'S BUSINESS

Balboa is an independent insurance agency. It sells all types of insurance--automobile, home, life, medical, and business. Its primary customer base is private individuals. One of Holmes's business plans is to expand the commercial insurance segment of the business. This was a partial motivation for her choosing an office in the central business area.

As an agent for several major insurance companies, Balboa is able to place each client with the insurer that best matches the client's needs. The business has four major applications--sales, claims assistance, client administration, and accounting.

SALES

Under Jack Triplett's administration, the sales cycle usually consisted of at least three parts. During the first segment, usually conducted at the client's office or residence, the agent gathers information about the client's insurance needs, income, and so on. Next, the agent takes the data back to Balboa's office for analysis. The agent then accesses one or more insurance carrier quotation systems to obtain the rates for several coverage options and to find the most cost effective plans. Finally, the agent returns to the client with one or more insurance proposals. The sales cycle is depicted in Figure 1-1. Triplett had not kept statistics regarding the effectiveness of this approach. Holmes, however, believed it contained a number of marketing flaws which she intended to correct.

On some occasions, the first proposal(s) delivered to the client was not satisfactory. Typically the client's concerns were that the premiums were too high or the coverage different from what the client wanted. Often this meant that Balboa's agent needed to go through another cycle of policy evaluations. Having an agent make multiple trips between the office and the client reduces the agent's efficiency. Holmes wanted to implement a system whereby Balboa's agent will meet with the client, access the insurance carriers' quotation systems as necessary, and arrive at a policy coverage during one client session.

The second flaw that Holmes perceived with Triplett's sales system was the interval between original client contact and the closure of a sale. Although she did not believe in high pressure tactics, her marketing instincts told her that the interval gave prospective clients an opportunity to contact other brokers or to change their mind completely. If the policy can be decided on and sold in one session, Balboa would be less likely to lose prospective clients. Furthermore, the brokers would have more time to pursue new business.

Because Balboa represents several insurance carriers, each of which has different options and incentives, it is difficult for Balboa's agents to know which carrier is best for a given client. Usually, the client's profile and desired coverages are submitted to at least two carriers to find the best coverage and premium. In the past this has been done by referencing quotation books. Currently, however, Balboa uses an office terminal to access a policy quotation system provided by each of the insurance carriers. Each of Triplett's offices had a dumb terminal and a modem for this purpose. The quotation systems are accessed via a switched communications line to a packet switching network service. The call goes to a local number, so there are no data communications line charges.

Figure 1-1. Balboa's Sales Cycle

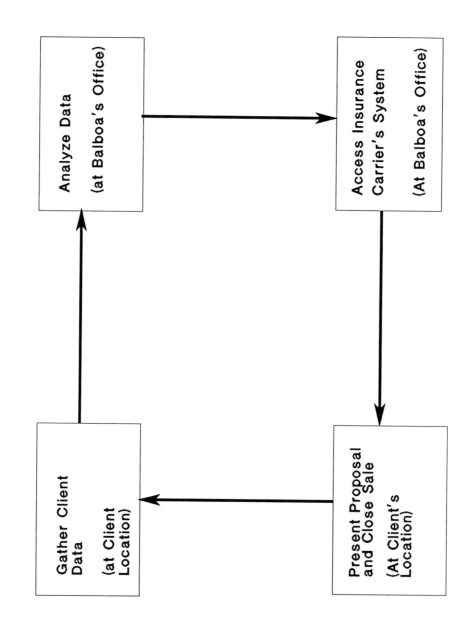

The only difficulty Balboa has experienced with the quotation system is that each company has its own data requirements and formats. That is, each carrier expects to receive data in a different order and most require at least one data item that the other carriers do not need. This disparity among carriers means that the agent must input much of the same data several times to obtain a quotation.

CLAIMS ASSISTANCE

Balboa does not process insurance claims, per se. The insurance carrier does all claims processing. However, the company does provide its clients with claims assistance. When one of Balboa's clients needs to make a claim, he or she typically begins the process by first contacting Balboa. In addition, Balboa is often contacted by people who have claims against Balboa's clients. For the most part, claims assistance consists of five activities: forms handling, coverage determination, explanation of claimant's rights and obligations, providing an interface between clients and carriers, and record keeping.

Balboa keeps copies of most forms needed to initiate a claim. For some clients, Balboa simply mails the necessary claim forms. These clients complete and mail the forms. In other instances, Balboa assists a client or claimant in completing the form and mailing the form to the insurance carrier or adjuster.

Many of Balboa's clients are not completely aware of their coverage details. Balboa assists these clients by reviewing their policies and explaining the client's coverage. This type of service is often a prelude to filing a claim. To determine the client's current coverage, Balboa's administrators sometimes need to access the database of the insurance company underwriting a policy. The office terminals are used to access these databases.

Similar to explaining the coverages, is the need to explain a claimant's rights and obligations. For example, many automobile policies provide a claimant with a rental car. However, restrictions to this coverage also apply. All of Balboa's insurance carriers have a maximum daily rental rate, limitations on mileage charges, and regulations for circumstances under which rental cars are provided, but these limits vary by insurance carrier and by policy. For example, suppose one of Balboa's clients is at fault in an automobile accident and that the client policy includes coverage for an automobile rental. Balboa's administrators or agents need to inform the claimant of the applicable rates and conditions; otherwise the claimant may incur un-reimbursable expenses.

Until clients submit a claim, they deal only with Balboa. Thus, many clients view Balboa as their insurer. When making claims, most clients prefer to deal with Balboa rather than with a large company in another city. Balboa's agents and administrators thus sometimes serve as the interface, or mediator, between the insurance carrier and a claimant or client.

Finally, Balboa keeps records for each claim that is filed. This information is used to help the agents sell additional coverage to clients and to help detect fraudulent claims. The format of this data is described below.

CLIENT ADMINISTRATION

Balboa maintains a database to keep track of clients, prospective clients, claimants, and insurance carriers. The database consists of both computerized and manually maintained files. Data in the database are updated whenever status changes occur, for example, payments, claims, cancellations, and so on.

In addition to the database, Balboa maintains a collection of form letters which are mail merged and sent to clients, prospective clients, and claimants. All these letters are maintained on one or more microcomputers. Examples of the letters stored include policy renewal letters, client personal history requests, and change in client status--marriage, birth, divorce, and so on.

ACCOUNTING

Like all companies, Balboa has financial related applications--accounts receivable, accounts payable, general ledger, payroll, budgeting, and so on. Under Jack Triplett, these applications were completely manual. Holmes intends to computerize most of the accounting functions.

ANTICIPATED APPLICATIONS

Holmes anticipates the need for a different marketing strategy if the business insurance segment of Balboa's business is to grow. Sales to individuals primarily requires one-on-one presentations for which professional presentation materials are not necessary. But marketing to a business will require that Balboa make formal presentations to business management. This means that Balboa must improve its presentation services. As a minimum, Holmes anticipates adding desk top publishing software, business graphics software, a color printer, and a plotter. These new resources need to be available to the entire staff.

THE BALBOA BUILDING

As mentioned above, Balboa has just moved into a renovated house in the downtown business district. Balboa is the only building occupant. The company has complete flexibility to modify the structure to meet its business needs. When the building was renovated, central air conditioning and heating were installed, and all the wiring was converted to provide grounded power outlets. Because the renovators assumed that the building would be used by a business, they wired each room with either two or three telephone outlets. The telephone outlets are connected to a wiring hub in a utility room on the main floor. The telephone wiring is standard telephone twisted wire pairs. The telephone receptacles in each room are standard RJ-11 connectors. During the renovation, no special accommodations were made for computing facilities. That is, no special wiring, air conditioning, or power outlets were installed.

The office building is a two story structure with a basement. The basement is not finished. It contains the furnace, hot water heater, and connections for a laundry room. Balboa plans to use the basement primarily for storage. The main floor houses the reception area, brokers' offices, and Barbara Holmes' office. The second floor has four rooms, two of which are occupied by office administrators. One administrator is always on duty in the reception area. The chief administrator, Rhonda Pagano, occupies one of the rooms, and the other two administrators, Sally Romansik and Marty Ahrens, share the other room. Usually either Romansik or Ahrens is on duty in the reception area.

COMPUTING AT BALBOA

Before consolidating the offices, Balboa was a not a heavy user of computing. One office had two microcomputers and the other had three. Each office had one dumb terminal with a modem for connecting to the insurance carriers' systems. All microcomputers were used in a stand-alone manner. That is, they were not interconnected and did not share printers or disks. Each microcomputer had its own printer. Two computers were connected to laser printers; the other printers were dot matrix. Jack Triplett's offices were relatively small; since only four people occupied each office, sharing computer resources and information was done by physically sharing a particular device. That is, if Rhonda Pagano needed to access Marty Ahrens' data or printer, she would use his computer. Balboa's terminal and computer configurations are given Figure 1-2.

Figure 1-2. Balboa's Terminal/Microcomputer Configuration

Terminal/Microcomputer Configuration	Number
Dumb terminal with modem	2
Microcomputer with laser printer	2
Microcomputer with dot matrix printer	3

The microcomputers were used primarily for word processing and for the mail merge application. Some client data are maintained on the micros, but the data are not well organized. On the microcomputers, each person kept his or her own files. These were either spreadsheet or word processing files, and the data were not usually shared among users. The primary data on clients and claims had been kept in paper format and stored in filing cabinets. Sharing this data among the staff in the small offices was not a problem because all employees and facilities were in close proximity to each other. Moreover, the office staff knew most of its clients personally; thus, inquiries were easily handled.

Each office was responsible for acquiring the software it needed. Fortunately, Jack Triplett had insisted on one restriction, that the software be compatible among the offices. That is, each office used the same word processing software, spreadsheet software, and so on. The number of copies acquired by each office was a factor over which each office had control, so there was no consistency between the offices. In one office, each microcomputer had its own word processing software installed on hard disks. In the other office the word processing program was kept on floppy disks and shared between the two systems. Thus, in that office, it was not possible for two people to use the word processing software concurrently.

THE PROBLEMS OF CONSOLIDATION

One of the strengths of the Balboa Insurance Agency was its personal, friendly service. This was partially made possible through the small office concept. After consolidation, it quickly became apparent that the larger, somewhat separated office space made the method of data and peripheral sharing described above inadequate. With offices on two floors, it was difficult for files to be shared among the office staff. Furthermore, with consolidation, the amount of data that needed to be maintained and shared was about twice the amount that was kept at each individual office. The additional data made it less likely that a client will be known to the person who happened to handle a client's request.

Another problem revolved around the use of software. Since there was not a copy of software for each system, sharing was more difficult, and it soon became apparent that each microcomputer needed constant access to frequently used software. Finding an unused copy was inconvenient and time consuming. Moreover, because the office administrators tended to work in both the office and reception area, it was important that they have access to their personal data files regardless of where they were working. With the situation that existed just after consolidation, this meant that all such files needed to be portable and hence kept on floppy disks.

In the smaller offices, two or three computers had been adequate. In the consolidated office, a computer or terminal was needed for each employee. With seven employees, Balboa was two microcomputers short of this ideal.

Most of the non-computerized data were kept in filing cabinets on the second floor. This made it difficult for brokers and the administrator in the reception area to access those data. Frequently client files were taken to a broker's office for examination or update. Because of the inconvenience of replacing the files, they often remained for some time in the office of the person last using the file. On these occasions one of the administrators would spend several minutes tracking down a missing file. Lack of easy accessibility also led to an increase in data duplication and reproduction costs. Holmes had detected several instances of inconsistent data due to data redundancy. On several occasions, agents had updated their personal client files and had neglected to pass the changes to the administrators for inclusion in the office files.

Holmes quickly realized that consolidation had a few drawbacks regarding the use of data and the computers. She did not want consolidation to change the personal, friendly reputation the firm had acquired over time. She wanted an agency which was very client oriented and where the office staff can quickly access data for any client with whom they were working. Holmes knew that Balboa needed some way to allow the office personnel to quickly share data. She guessed that two hours of productivity per day was being lost while staff searched for data or programs. Not all of this time was spent looking for data. As a result of searching for items, the amount of casual conversation in the office had increased.

Holmes did not know how the information problem could be solved or how much it would cost. After the expense of acquiring the company and consolidating the offices, Balboa's cash position could not support an expensive solution. Holmes figured that immediately she could budget approximately $12,000 to solve what she referred to as the "computer and data problem."

FINDING SOLUTIONS

Nobody working for Balboa knew how to solve the information flow problem. Joe Barton, one of the broker/agents, suggested she contact one of their clients, Paul Martinez, to get some help. Martinez taught data processing at the local community college and was president of a local computer users' group. He was often called on to help people having microcomputer problems. Holmes arranged a meeting with Martinez. Prior to the meeting she drafted a brief outline of the problem as she perceived it. Her outline is shown in Figure 1-3.

Figure 1-3. Outline of Balboa's Computer Configuration and Concerns

I.   Equipment
       a) Five IBM compatible microcomputers - 2 XTs and 3 ATs, all with hard
           disk drives
       b) Two laser printers
       c) Three dot matrix printers
       d) Two terminals
       e) Two modems

II.   Office
       a) Two story building
       b) Offices on both levels
       c) Flexibility to make changes

III.   Personnel
       a) President
       b) Three broker/agents
       c) Three office administrators
           Little computer expertise except as competent users in specialized areas,
           for example, word processing

IV.   Concerns
       a) **Major: Data availability**. Data in filing cabinets are not readily available
           or sharable. Each computer has its own set of files. Office staff can only
           access files by physically using the machine on which they are kept or by
           storing data on diskettes.

       b) **Major: Printer conflict**. Each computer has an attached printer, but it
           is not always the type the user needs. The laser printers are used for all
           external communication. These printers are attached to computers in the
           second floor administration offices where the brokers find it difficult to
           get access to them. Because the per-page cost of the laser printers are
           greater than that for the dot matrix printers, it is more economical for

draft documents to be printed on the dot matrix printers. The administration staff does much of the draft copy work, but, with one exception, they do not have easy access to a dot matrix printer. The printers attached to two of the administration computers are laser printers. Moving to a dot matrix printer is inconvenient for small print jobs.

c) **Major: Remote sites.** How can brokers prepare a proposal at a customer's location? Moreover, can this be done without the broker having to enter the data separately for each insurance carrier?

d) **Minor: Software sharing.** Software fits into two categories--the programs everyone uses frequently and the programs that a few people use occasionally. For software in the first category, we have already made sure that one copy was available for each computer. For software in the second category, there are only one or two copies. Thus, if someone needs to use software in the second category, he or she must find an unused copy. The unused copies are supposed to be checked out and in from a convenient, central location; in reality that seldom happens. Usually the copies were found in the office of the person using the software last.

e) **Minor: Data protection.** I have a few files that I consider sensitive and do not want available to my employees. Specifically, I want to protect data about salaries and Balboa's financial position. I have been keeping this data on flexible disks that are kept locked in my filing cabinet--a practical, but sometimes inconvenient solution.

f) **Minor: Equipment.** There are not enough computers for each employee to have a dedicated machine. Currently, the three brokers are sharing one microcomputer. The output devices are incapable of supporting the colored output that we think will be effective for presentations to prospective business clients.

V.   Cost
        The solutions to these problems should cost no more than $12,000 (and preferably less).

VI.   Schedule
        An immediate solution, say within three to six months, is desired.

Martinez immediately recognized Balboa's problem as a computer resource sharing problem that several small companies had asked him about in the past. He also found it interesting that the problem was coming up more frequently. In Meridian, most small companies that lacked computer support from a larger organization had purchased microcomputers to support their business. Many of these businesses had eventually purchased several microcomputers. After using the machines in a stand-alone manner for some time, these users often came to the realization that they could work more efficiently and economically if they could share disk drives, printers, and data. Frequently a business arrived at this conclusion when they needed to purchase a new system or, as in Balboa's case, when they reorganized the office. Because Martinez had encountered this situation before, he had some ready alternatives.

Martinez's solutions fell into four basic categories: a central computer with terminals, a local area network (LAN), a sub-local area network (sub-LAN), and a service bureau.

THE CENTRAL COMPUTER ALTERNATIVE

When Martinez first mentioned a central computer multi-user solution, Holmes's first reaction was that it would be too expensive. She had the image of a minicomputer with terminals, complicated operations, new, expensive hardware and software, and a major re-learning effort so the staff could use the new hardware and software. Martinez acknowledged that such a system was an option, but that there was also a more palatable solution.

Several years ago, a multi-user computer system did mean something beyond a microcomputer-based system. However, with today's high performance systems based on the latest microprocessors, a microcomputer equipped with the right operating system can provide multi-user capabilities. Most importantly for Balboa, this solution can also provide complete compatibility with IBM DOS software. Thus, Balboa's investment in software and training will be protected.

The key to such a multi-user system is the operating system. The hardware can be an off-the-shelf microcomputer as long as it has sufficient memory, disk space, and speed to support multiple users. However, the operating system must be able to support multiple concurrent users, display devices, and peripherals. The DOS operating system currently being run on Balboa's microcomputers cannot support this type of processing but several such operating systems exist.

A company just beginning to acquire a multi-user system, would need to acquire a high performance microcomputer, a multi-user operating system, asynchronous terminals, and the microcomputer application software. A diagram of such a configuration is shown in Figure 1-4. With this type of system, the per-user cost is relatively low because each user does not need a dedicated microcomputer. Instead, they can use a much less expensive terminal to access the system.

The disadvantage of such systems is that they are not nearly so developed as LAN technology. First, the number of concurrent users is more limited than for most LAN implementations. Some of the systems are unable to support the current number of terminal and microcomputers at Balboa. Most of the systems that can support all of Balboa's users have limited expansion ability. Second, the operating systems are generally weak in the area of file protection and concurrent access to files. Third, the typical communication links to the central computer is quite low, 19.2 K bits per second (bps) or lower. However, this does not tend to be a major problem with this configuration because the only data communications traffic is for display on the monitor. That is, programs and data files are not down-loaded. Fourth, use of pointing devices like a mouse is not supported. This restricts the use of a number of programs, particularly graphics software. The attraction of this solution is greater for new computer users than for Balboa because of the low per-user cost. For new users, the average cost per user workstation can be less than the cost of individual microcomputers connected to a LAN. Except for the central host, the other workstations can be inexpensive display devices.

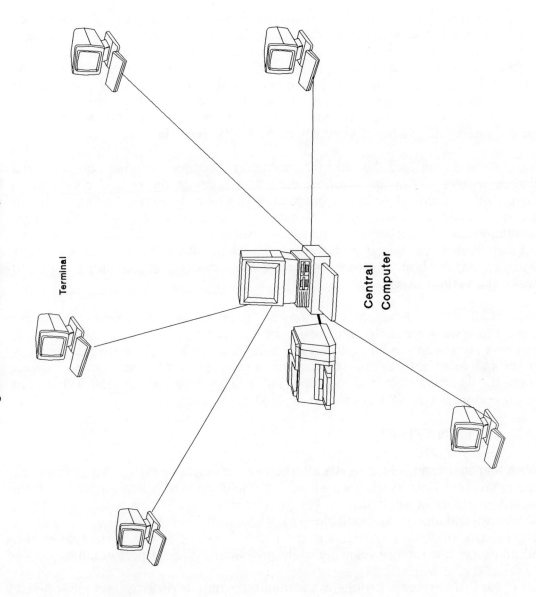

Figure 1-4. A Multi-user System

Terminal

Central
Computer

15

In Balboa's case, an initial investment in microcomputers has already been made, but their microcomputers can be connected to a central system using a terminal emulation program. Thus, their workstations can operate in a stand-alone mode or can connect to the central system; however, they cannot do both at the same time. The two terminals that have been used only to access insurance carrier systems can also be integrated into the system to provide each employee with his or her own terminal or microcomputer. The total cost of this solution for hardware and the operating system software is well within Balboa's budget.

A variation of the central computer solution is that of clustered microcomputers. With this solution, each user accesses the central computer as above, with a terminal or microcomputer. The host, however, has an on-board processor board for each user. This is illustrated in Figure 1-5. Each user essentially has his or her own microprocessor and copy of DOS. The host's peripherals, disk drives and printers, are shared by all users. As with the above configuration, the host computer itself must use a customized operating system to service the various users.

Both of the above configurations are ideal for remote access. Users can access the system remotely and obtain the full power of the system because all programs are run at the host. In a LAN configuration wherein software programs are down-loaded into a workstation, remote access is possible but not always practical. The time required to down-load a large program, say 250 K bytes, at typical remote access speeds of 1200 or 2400 bps is excessive.

LAN ALTERNATIVES

When Martinez explained the LAN alternatives, he began by saying that perhaps the biggest problem Holmes will face with a LAN solution is selecting one system from the large number of alternatives. The possibilities range over a wide spectrum of speed, cost, and number of available work stations. If Holmes chooses this solution, her objective must be to select an option that is cost effective and capable of a certain amount of future expansion while providing sufficient performance.

All LAN implementations, at the minimum, require an investment in software and cables. Many require additional hardware as well. Martinez briefly explained

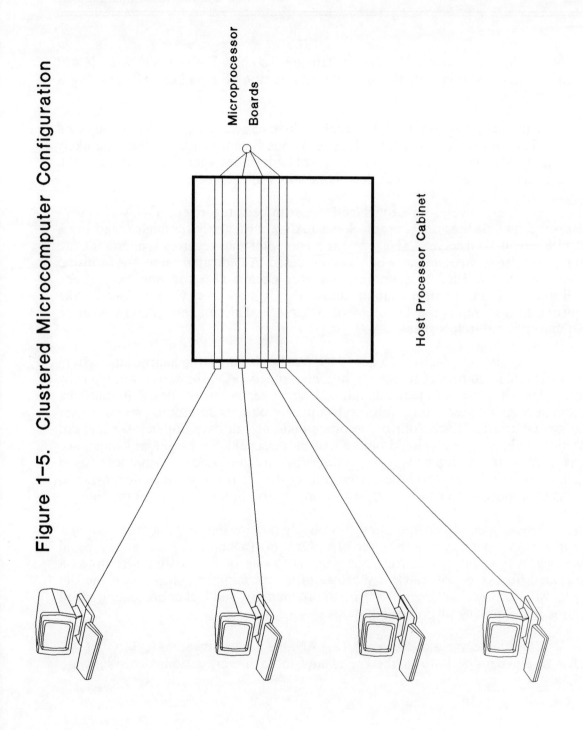

Figure 1-5. Clustered Microcomputer Configuration

Microprocessor Boards

Host Processor Cabinet

17

to Holmes how a LAN would work at Balboa. To show Holmes how a LAN will meet her needs, Martinez drew a possible configuration for Balboa. His drawing is shown in Figure 1-6.

If Balboa implements a LAN, each of its microcomputers will be connected by some kind of wiring. For a LAN the size Balboa is contemplating, the most likely medium is twisted wire pairs. The wires might be installed specifically for the LAN, but it is possible that the existing telephone wires might work.

There are several ways in which LANs can be categorized. One way is with respect to how devices are shared. Some LANs, particularly the high speed ones, require a dedicated server. The server is a computer that receives requests for file and/or printer services and acts on those requests. A dedicated server performs no other functions. That is, a dedicated server cannot also function as a user's workstation. Other implementations allow one or more user workstations on the network to also fulfill the functions of a server. This implementation is more commonly found in low speed LANs.

Regardless of which of the above approaches is taken, the heart of the system will be the file and printer server(s). In a high speed LAN, the server will typically be a relatively powerful microcomputer. The server holds all files that must be shared among the users. It will also collect printer outputs and route them to a user designated printer. Each floor of the office building can have both a laser and dot matrix printer to which printed output can be directed. Each user will thus have easy access to whichever type of printer he or she needs. Moreover, each workstation can have its own dedicated printer if necessary. Holmes, for instance, can have a local printer in her office to print payroll and financial information.

A dedicated server solution will probably require that Balboa acquire a new computer to operate as a file server. One of Balboa's AT machines could conceivably function in that role; however, using one of the existing systems as a dedicated file server will cause a shortage of microcomputers. Moreover, the file server will likely need a larger disk drive, more memory, and higher processing speed than is found on any of Balboa's systems.

If the file server is the heart of the LAN, the LAN software is its brain. LAN software must reside both in the server and in each workstation. This software

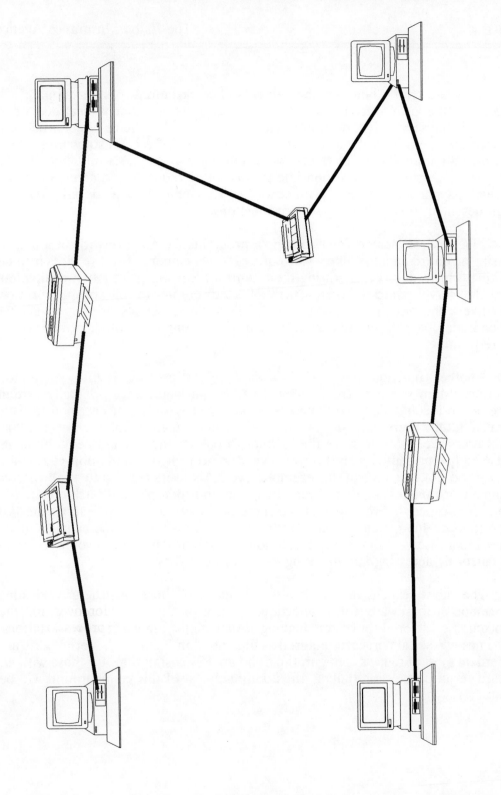

Figure 1-6. LAN Configuration

directs the data traffic between the server and workstations. For example, in a workstation, the LAN software will direct file requests to either a local disk or to disks on the file server. The software that does this is called the re-director because it redirects requests from the local system to the server. The LAN software running in a workstation also provides the software interface to the LAN medium. In the server, the LAN software is responsible for accepting requests and acting on them. The requests can be for file or print services. The server uses a special operating system designed to expedite the service functions.

File services include down-loading a program, accessing records in a file, or accessing an entire data file, like a word processing document. Print services include accepting print requests and storing them until the current print job is completed. Then, the server typically writes the collected output to the proper printer; alternatively, the print job might be retained on the server for printing at a later time or it may be both printed and retained for printing on another printer or for later re-printing.

Another function the LAN software might provide is file contention resolution. Many of the microcomputer software packages were originally written to operate in a stand-alone environment. That is, they were not designed to have several different users accessing a file at the same time. LANs, however, allow several users access to the same file. Although the advent of shared environments like LANs has prompted some software vendors to provide contention resolution, some still do not. At Balboa, for example, two LAN users could potentially access the same word processing document, change it, and then place it back on the file server. If two people are updating the same document at the same time, the last person to place the document back on the file server will erase the changes made by the other user. Contention resolution capabilities prohibit two users from simultaneously accessing and updating the same record or file.

The least expensive LAN alternatives are those which use existing microcomputer hardware for connection. Most of these alternatives use the microcomputer's serial port for making connections among the workstations. Sometimes two serial ports are required as illustrated in Figure 1-7. Serial ports are standard on most of today's configurations and are low cost options for those without standard serial ports. For Balboa, the additional cost of this configuration will be

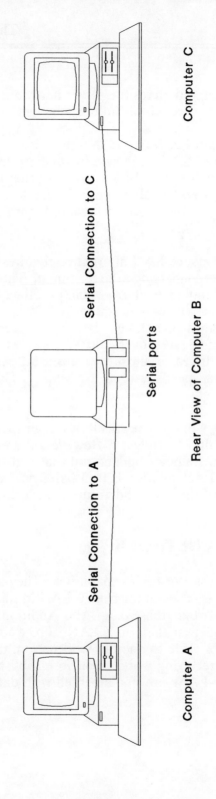

Figure 1-7. LAN Connection Using Two Serial Ports

cables, LAN software, and perhaps file server hardware and printer controllers. All can be purchased for a price within Balboa's budget.

The major disadvantage of LANs that use serial ports for the medium interface is speed. In general, such systems operate at speeds under 100,000 bps; many have a maximum speed of 19.2 Kbps. In general, low speed LANs function well for small file transfers, database record access, and printer output. But they perform poorly in a shared environment where large files and programs are down-loaded.

A higher performance LAN alternative requires that each workstation have a LAN adapter card for connecting to the medium. These logic cards cost anywhere from approximately $200 to well over $500. However, like the cost of many electronics components, the cost of these boards is coming down. The benefit gained from high performance LANS is higher speeds. At the low end, these systems provide transfer rates over 100,000 bps, as fast or faster than locally connected floppy disk drives. Typically, speeds are 1 Mbps or higher. At the upper end of the scale, data speeds exceed 10 Mbps. The industry trend is toward increasingly higher speeds.

Some of the LAN options, particularly a high speed LAN with a powerful file server, are beyond Balboa's budget. However, there is a wide variety of LAN options that are within Balboa's budget and that will satisfy Balboa's needs. One major advantage of a LAN solution is transparency. All file and printer sharing is done almost as though the files and printers were locally attached to the user's workstation.

SUB-LOCAL AREA NETWORK

Sub-LANs provide a subset of LAN capabilities. They allow peripheral sharing and file transfer capabilities. They differ from a LAN in that a sub-LAN's data transfer rates and costs are lower than those of a LAN. Additionally, file transfer capabilities are typically less transparent than on a LAN. For example, on most sub-LANs, if a user needs to transfer a file to another workstation, the sender must first call the person operating the receiving workstation to establish the software environment for data transfer. Sub-LANs are implemented with data switches.

Data switches provide connection between microcomputers in much the same way a telephone company provides connections between callers. A switch configuration is shown in Figure 1-8. In the figure, if device A needs to connect with device B, the switch will establish the connection as illustrated in Figure 1-9. Many data switches are designed specifically for sharing peripheral devices like printers and plotters and use manual switching. That is, a user needs to turn a switch selector knob on the switch box to make the proper connection. Some of the more advanced switches allow switching via keyboard commands and support file transfers and modem pooling. With keyboard command switching, a user can enter the address of a device to which it needs to connect. If the device is not already in use, the connection is made. The connection remains until one of the two stations requests a disconnect; alternatively, a disconnect may occur after a specified time of inactivity. Keyboard command switching does not solve the file transfer problem described above. Operators at the sending and receiving computers must coordinate the file transfer by starting the file transfer software at each end of the connection. Modem pooling at Balboa will allow a user at a microcomputer to connect to one of the two available modems via the data switch. He or she could then access an insurance carrier's quotation system or database.

This type of configuration is relatively inexpensive as the connection between microcomputers and the switch is usually made through the computer's existing serial port and because the switch itself is relatively inexpensive. A switch to accommodate all of Balboa's devices together with the necessary file transfer software can be purchased for less than $2500. This solution has the lowest cost of all the alternatives.

The disadvantages of a data switch are the speed of the communications link, lack of user transparency, and contention. The line speeds supported are typically 19.2 Kbps or lower. This speed is adequate for small file transfers but not for large ones such as down-loading program files. Peripheral sharing is simple and straight-forward. File transfers are more difficult.

A file transfer is effected with software operating in conjunction with the data switch. Microcomputer software which allows files to be transferred between two computers over a serial connection can be purchased for approximately $100. The data switch provides the connection between sending and receiving computers. The difficulty in transferring a file lies in the fact that the computer user at each end of

Figure 1-8. A Sub-LAN Configuration

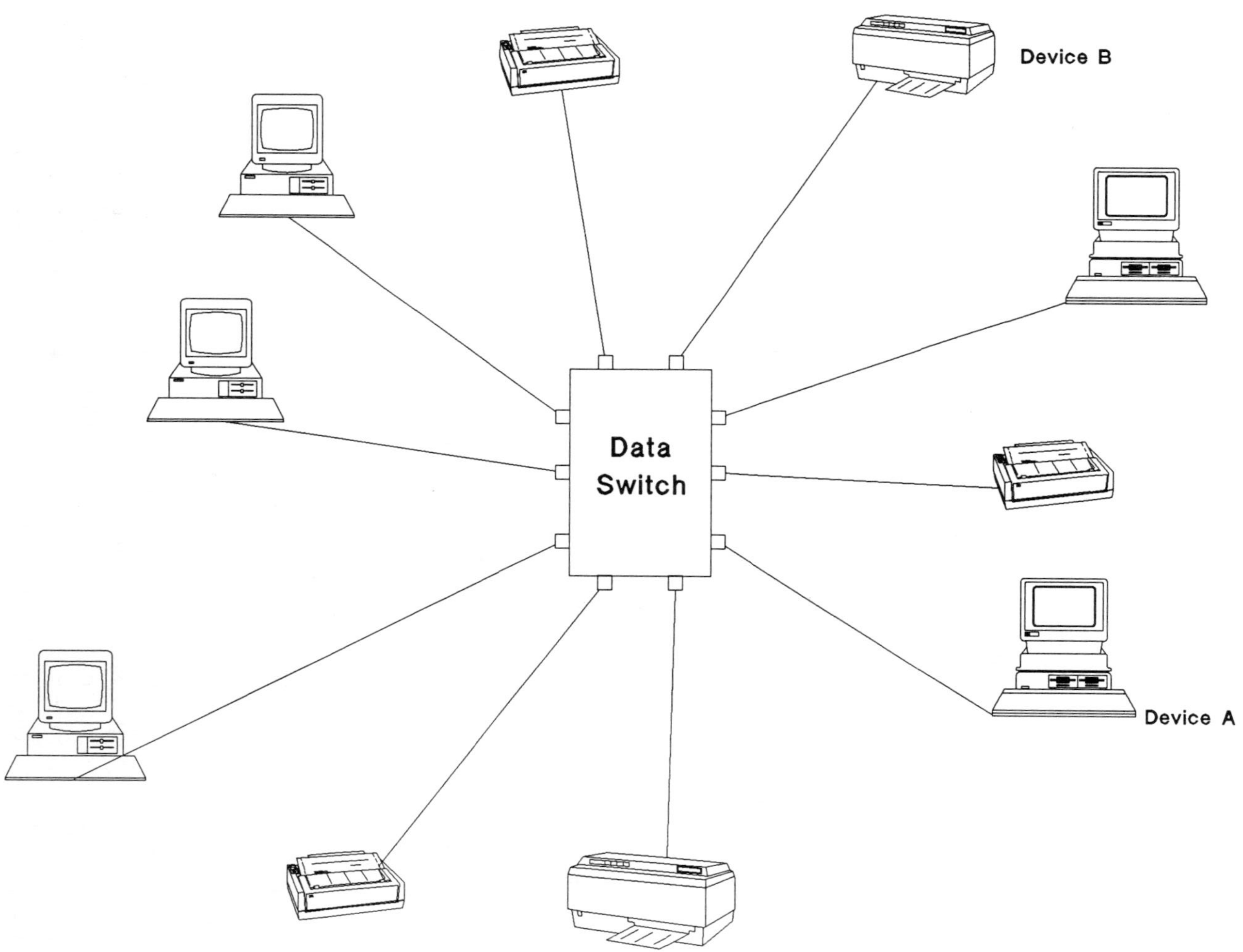

Figure 1-9. Data Switch Connection in a Sub-LAN Configuration

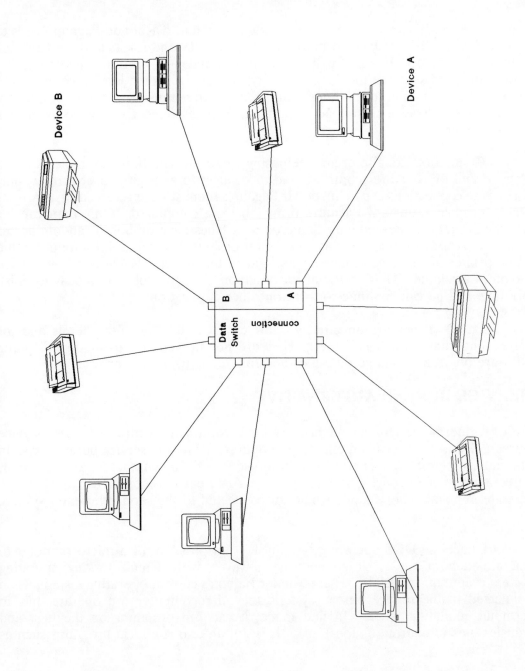

25

the transfer must start the file transfer program. Thus, if Rhonda Pagano needs to send a file to Holmes, Pagano must first call Holmes and ask her to start the file transfer program. Holmes will need to suspend her current microcomputer application and start the file transfer utility. Pagano will then issue a command to connect her computer to Holmes's, and initiate the transfer. Upon completion, Pagano would issue a disconnect command, or a disconnect would occur after a timeout interval.

Contention can also occur when using a data switch. If, for example, Rhonda Pagano and Marty Ahrens both wanted to connect to a specific laser printer, only one of the connections can be made. If Pagano's request were received first, Ahrens would need to wait until Pagano's print job were completed. Only then can his connection request be granted. Some data switches have on-board random access memory (RAM) to alleviate this contention problem. If multiple outputs for the same printer are received, one can be held in the switch's RAM until the device becomes available. Thus, in the above situation, Ahrens's job will appear to finish printing, and he can continue to work on other applications.

Data switches are an effective, low cost way to share peripherals and for infrequent transfers of small files. They are not so well suited for down-loading software programs or large data files and for frequent file exchanges.

SERVICE BUREAU ALTERNATIVE

Another alternative Holmes might consider is contracting with a computer service bureau. Data sharing can be effected via data stored on the service bureau's system (the host system). Balboa will be able to use its existing computers and terminals to connect to the service bureau's system. Also, each computer can continue to operate in a stand-alone mode when not connected to the service bureau's system.

Under the DOS operating system, it is not possible for a microcomputer to operate in both modes simultaneously; however, with a multi-tasking operating system even that is possible. That is, under Balboa's current operating system, when connected to the service bureau system, the microcomputer can operate only in terminal emulation mode. In that mode, it can run programs on the host and transfer files to or from its local disk. It is not able to run local programs such as word processing or spread sheet applications while connected to the host. Likewise, when operating in stand-alone mode, it is not possible to access the host to transfer files. With a multi-tasking operating system, local applications can run concurrently with host access.

Connection to the host might be made via the computer's serial port to a statistical multiplexer. This will allow each microprocessor access to the host at any time while minimizing line costs. Provided the service bureau is located in the local calling area, the line costs will not be too great. Moreover, management and support of all but the local components of such a system will not be Balboa's responsibility.

On the negative side, this solution does not provide some of the capabilities Balboa needs. First, although data files can be easily shared, program files pose a problem. Down-loading programs from the host over a typical communications link of 9,600 bps will be quite slow. At that speed, a 250,000 byte program will take a minimum of 4.3 minutes. That figure assumes 100% line utilization for data, an unrealistic assumption. Thus, the link is most useful only for exchanging rather small data files. Program files will still need to reside either locally on each system or be programs which run on the host. For example, the client database could be maintained entirely on the host using the host's database management system and host resident programs. Naturally, the more the resources of the host are used, the greater the cost to Balboa.

Martinez summarized the options available to Holmes. His summary is shown in Figure 1-10.

Figure 1-10. Balboa's Alternatives

1. Continue as is.
2. Continue mostly as is, but provide better organization and data flow.
3. Use a central multi-user system.
4. Use a data switch to form a sub-LAN.
5. Implement a LAN.
6. Contract with a service bureau.

IMPLEMENTATION CONCERNS

Holmes was fairly optimistic when Martinez finished his explanation of how her computer problem could be resolved. However, she was not quite prepared for what he had to say next. Martinez pointed out that installing one of the above solutions was relatively easy. However, two things that many users of shared systems like a LAN or multi-user system soon discovered are (1) that they were not well prepared to manage such a system and (2) that the hardware and installation costs were not the only costs incurred.

Holmes at first could not envision any problems. Her staff will be using the same software products, and the system will make the fact that files and programs were resident on another computer somewhat transparent. Where could the problems lie? Martinez told her what she should expect by first reviewing how things currently work at Balboa. He used a LAN implementation as a model to contrast how things might work if one of the above solutions were adopted.

Each employee has his or her own system, and each is responsible for operating that system. Two of the major operations tasks are (1) making backup copies of files, and (2) when a disk becomes full, the person responsible for the system removes any files that are no longer needed and backs up and then removes those that need to be saved.

Reliability of Balboa's computers is not currently a problem. If one of the microcomputers malfunctions, only the person using that machine is inconvenienced. Other employees are able to continue their work without disruption.

Management of a LAN, even a small one like the one Balboa might implement, is time consuming. One of the biggest changes between a LAN and several stand-alone systems is that someone needs to be responsible for the LAN. That is, to provide efficient, continuous service, there ought to be a LAN manager/operator. Although this is not a full time function for a small LAN, it does take extra time and expertise. For a large LAN, the system management tasks can be a full-time job. Converting to a shared system carries with it an entirely new set of responsibilities.

LAN MANAGEMENT RESPONSIBILITIES

Holmes had started the meeting hoping for a simple technical solution to her computer problem. The technical solutions to her original concept of the problem were indeed simple and affordable. What she had not counted on was the other problems the solution carried with it. Martinez continued to explain the impact of the proposed solutions by suggesting some areas that needed resolution before adopting a shared user environment. Some of these issues are listed below. In his suggestions, he again used a LAN implementation as an example; however, the issues apply to any of the above solutions.

1. **System administration.** Since a LAN requires shared devices such as printers, printer controllers, and one or more servers, someone must be responsible for caring for them. Files on the server need to be backed up periodically. If the disk becomes full, someone must be responsible for removing or archiving files. New files and programs must occasionally be added to the system. Individual user directories need to be created. Security measures must be imposed. Batch files need to be created to provide a variety of functions such as user login, DOS search paths, and so on. At Balboa, there are several unanswered questions such as: Who will be responsible for assigning file and user security? Who will install new versions of the file server's operating system? Who will be responsible for upgrading the LAN software on each individual system? Who will connect new systems and LAN devices? Who will report problems to the vendors? Although the LAN administrator does not need to be a computer expert, he or she must at least be a

super user and have an aptitude for technical details. Martinez indicated that if the LAN administrator came from Balboa's current staff, Holmes will likely have to send him or her through several weeks of training.

2. **Training**. The LAN manager needs to know enough about the system to add new users, install operating systems, gather information regarding problems, and even solve problems of a local nature. None of Balboa's current employees has the necessary expertise to fulfill the role of LAN manager. Martinez also indicated that it will be prudent to have at least two people capable of performing such functions. With two people, it will be more likely that at least one person is available when problems occur.

Moreover, Martinez indicated that the users will also need some additional training. For instance, they will need to know how to route their print outputs to the proper printer and how to log on to the system. Although for the most part, users will use the system in much the same way as before, using it will not be completely transparent. Some of the solutions, like a sub-LAN, require completely new operating procedures. A few hours of education for each employee will be necessary.

3. **Maintenance**. Balboa does not carry a maintenance contract on any of its equipment. If a printer or computer breaks, it is taken to a local computer store for repair. Sometimes, the repair might take a week, but the loss of one microcomputer or printer for that amount of time is not too disruptive. However, if the file server fails and is out of service for a week, what would the effect be on Balboa's business? Each of the workstations could, of course, continue operating in a stand-alone mode. However, the files and programs on the file server will not be available. The printers will be available only if reconnected directly to an individual work station.

If the system fails, someone must gather the problem details and either fix the problem or call someone to make the repairs. Even if the file server never has a problem, there are numerous small maintenance and operations tasks which must be done--changing ribbons and toner cartridges, keeping a stock of paper, maintaining the copies of the disk backups, keeping software and documentation current, interfacing with suppliers, and so on. Under the current mode of operation, each of these responsibilities are distributed among all the employees.

Because of the critical nature of shared hardware like a LAN server or data switch, Martinez suggested that Balboa consider placing that equipment under a maintenance agreement. This was a recurring cost Holmes had not counted on.

4. **Software**. All the software Balboa had acquired were stand-alone versions. In all cases, the software vendors had network versions available. All of Balboa's software vendors allowed their customers to upgrade stand-alone versions for a network licensed version. Usually the software vendors levied a modest charge for the upgrade and corresponding documentation. Balboa was fortunate in this regard. Some software vendors do not have an upgrade policy. Their customers must purchase a completely new network version of the software without receiving credit for the software they have already purchased.

Once received, the software needs to be installed, individual or corporate configurations established, and then the software installation tested to ensure that it operates correctly. Even if doing all of the above is not complex, it does tend to be time consuming.

5. **Communications Speed**. Holmes needs to decide how the computer solution will be used immediately and predict how it will likely be used in the future. These characteristics help determine the correct alternative and associated communications speed. Some solutions to the immediate problem may be unsatisfactory for future needs. If system use will be primarily to access records and small word processing documents, then a lower speed between the server and workstations will be adequate. If large programs are to be down-loaded from a shared disk, then higher speeds, are essential. If several new users are likely to be added, or if the existing users will be frequently accessing a shared disk concurrently, then the speed of the communications link should be relatively high. Of the proposed options, the general speed categories and their effectiveness are shown in Figure 1-11.

Figure 1-11. Comparison of Data Communications Speeds

Speed Range	Effectiveness
Under 20 Kbps	Adequate for light usage and transfers of small files.
20 K to 100 Kbps	Adequate for concurrent usage and transfers of small files.
100 K to 1 Mbps	Adequate for performance equivalent to a floppy disk for several concurrent users. Adequate for down-loading most program files and large data files.
1 M to 4 Mbps	Better performance than the preceding and better able to accommodate multiple users and future expansion.
Above 4 Mbps	Superior performance, but at an increased cost.

6. **Communication with Insurance Carriers**. Martinez next asked how Balboa proposed handling communication with the insurance carriers. Balboa can operate in the current mode using the two terminals and modems. Alternatively, a shared system ought to be able to accommodate modem pooling and switched data communications with Balboa's insurance carriers. A LAN can do this by having the modems attached to the server. An employee can then establish a connection from his or her work station through the server. Thus, it will not be necessary for an employee to move to one of the terminals to prepare a quote. An added benefit is that Balboa can use a standard input form and have a program translate the data into the formats required by individual carriers. Some programming work will need

to be done if the common format approach is used. Balboa will need to contract with someone to get the program written.

At the conclusion of the meeting, Martinez admitted that to some extent he had been playing the devil's advocate in discussing the problems inherent in shared systems. For most users shared systems are cost effective. The major investment in time and training tends to occur when the system is new. Once things settle down, the amount of time required to manage a system of Balboa's size ought to be relatively small. However, he told Holmes that he wanted to stress that too often users fail to consider these consequences of creating a shared user environment.

Holmes came away from the meeting with Martinez less enthusiastic about finding an easy solution to the computer problem. She knew that technically it was possible, but she worried about the expertise necessary to operate such a system and the time it would take to administer it. She wondered if one or two of the current administrative staff were interested and capable of managing a shared system and how much time will be lost from his or her other duties. If she needed to hire another person part time to do the computer related work, will the solution be cost effective? She also wondered if the time lost through system management will be compensated for by increased productivity among other employees. She realized that a solution would require a great deal more planning and evaluation than she had thus far given it.

About the only thing Holmes was sure of after the meeting with Martinez was that she did not care for the service bureau alternative. She did not see that mode of operation as an improvement over the current situation, the cost factor was too open ended, and Balboa will lose some of the control over its data processing. Any solution would need to come from the other alternatives.

YOU MAKE THE DECISIONS

Suppose that you were hired by Holmes to recommend a solution to Balboa's computer and data problem. Prepare a proposal by completing one or more of the following exercises.

1. Summarize the options available to solve the problem. Do not fail to include the current system and variations of the current system as options.

2. Can you think of any solutions to the problem other than those presented in Paul Martinez's analysis? What are they? Can any of the proposed alternatives be integrated into one solution? If so, describe the systems; if not, explain why.

3. Complete the following matrix for the solutions.

	Cost/ user	Speed	Ease of Management	Ease of Use	Soln to Problem
Multi-user					
Sub-LAN (Data switch)					
LAN Serial port					
Low speed LAN LAN card					
High speed LAN LAN card					

Give the best solution a rating of 1 and the worst solution a rating of 5. For the most accurate estimates, use current cost and speed figures. Good sources for such material are periodicals such as *Byte*, *Computerworld*, *PC Magazine*, and *PC World*. In the absence of such research, use the figures given in the casebook appendix. If you did exercise 1 or 2, add your alternative solutions to the matrix.

Based on your completed matrix, which solution seems to be best? Draw a diagram of the system configuration. What type of wiring does your solution require? Can the existing telephone wires be used? Rank each of the solutions from the above matrix in order from best to worst.

4. Assume that Barbara Holmes selects one of the above solutions to the problem. How should she address the issue of system administration? Who in the office are the best candidates for the administrator position? That is, should administrators or agents be selected for the task? Explain your decision.

5. Can LAN administration be done effectively by a part-time employee? What are the advantages and disadvantages (both technical and business) of a part-time LAN administrator?

6. For each technical solution, work out a cost analysis and determine the payback period. Make and document the necessary assumptions to complete this analysis. Will a technical solution to Balboa's problem be cost effective (assuming that the solution does not exceed the budgeted amount)?

7. Besides a data communications system, are there applications that Balboa needs to solve the information problem? What are the major application needs? How will these application solutions interface with the data communications solution.

8. Each of the technical solutions introduces a single point of failure. For instance, if the server malfunctions in the LAN solution or if the data switch breaks with the sub-LAN solution, Balboa will lose a significant portion of its computing capability. How serious do you think this problem is? What can be done to minimize the effects of this? What are the cost factors for these solutions?

9. With a LAN solution, there are many available options. Some LANs provide a peer protocol. A peer protocol allows data stored at any node to be accessed by other nodes; therefore, these LANs do not require a dedicated server. Other implementations require a dedicated server. Compare and contrast these alternatives. Which would you recommend for Balboa? Why did you make your choice?

10. The performance of a LAN is closely tied to the speed of the LAN and the speed of the file server's disk drives. How do each of these influence LAN performance? Assume three of Balboa's employees each attempt to down-load a 250,000 byte file at the same time. A file this size can be loaded into the computer's RAM from a flexible disk in approximately 3 seconds. What is the minimum LAN speed necessary to provide performance equal to a local flexible disk? Assume that the LAN overhead is 25% of the carrying capacity.

11. Under what circumstances will a central multi-user host system be the most effective?

12. Under what circumstances will a sub-LAN system be the most effective?

13. Under what circumstances will a LAN with peer workstations (see question 9) be the most effective?

14. Under what circumstances will a LAN system with a dedicated file server be the most effective?

15. Under what circumstances will a LAN system using serial connections running at 19.2 Kbps be the most effective?

16. Under what circumstances will a LAN system operating at 1 Mbps be the most effective?

17. Under what circumstances will a LAN system operating at 10 Mbps be the most effective?

18. Which of the characteristics in questions 11-17 most closely match Balboa's processing needs?

NORTHERN STATE UNIVERSITY

CASE OBJECTIVES

Sometimes organizations procure computing equipment to satisfy specific needs. In some of these instances, the organization has ended up with a variety of stand-alone systems. With today's technology, it is relatively easy to network a variety of hardware, but networking the software is usually not so easy. In this case study, you will see how one organization found itself with several different computing installations and how the disparity among the installations led to additional expense and lack of communication among the organization's groups. this case you will evaluate the following:

. The problems arising when a variety of computer equipment is used to solve an organization's problems.

. The problems of integrating heterogeneous hardware and software.

. Solutions to integrating different systems into one network.

. Management issues regarding acquiring and networking computers.

NORTHERN STATE UNIVERSITY - AN INTRODUCTION

Northern State University (NSU) has a long and distinguished history. Founded as an agricultural college, it has established a world-wide reputation as an agricultural and engineering school. NSU has also gained regional recognition for its business and science programs. It grants graduate degrees in business and the sciences as well as in agriculture and engineering.

COMPUTING AT NSU - AN OVERVIEW

NSU has recently realized it has a major computer problem, an unmanaged proliferation of islands of computing. "Islands of computing" refers to the situation where several colleges and departments have independently procured computing equipment to support their academic and research programs. Although some of these academic units have formed local networks of the computers it controls, campus wide, these networks are not interconnected. This has resulted in isolated islands of computing networks. This problem is an indirect consequence of three general trends--computerization, expansion, and unification--and a direct consequence of the computer technology explosion.

The General Events - Computerization

NSU was one of the first universities to integrate the use of computers into its curriculum. Its first academic computing system was installed in 1955. Since that time, a variety of equipment has been used to promote teaching and research. The computers in use today cover the entire spectrum of power and capability. The hardware, obtained from a variety of vendors, includes microcomputers, minicomputers, mainframes, and a scientific computer. Some of the equipment was purchased from department or college funds, some was bought with research grants, and some was donated by the computer companies.

An individual college or department at NSU can acquire equipment to support its academic or research programs if it has the funds or can obtain corporate donations. These purchases do not need approval of NSU's administration. Equipment falling under this category consists primarily of microcomputers, minicomputers, and super-minicomputers because departments and colleges typically do not have the resources to obtain larger systems. The large mainframe systems and the scientific computer are centrally purchased by NSU. This uncontrolled expansion capability led to the problem that will soon be described in detail.

The General Events - Expansion

Like many colleges and universities, NSU experienced a rapid expansion starting in the early 1960s. During this period, which lasted for approximately 15 years, NSU expanded both its facilities and its programs. New buildings were erected, graduate degrees were added in several areas, the enrollment nearly doubled to approximately 24,000 students, and the faculty grew at a comparable rate.

During this period of expansion, NSU also opened three campus extension facilities in the state's major urban centers. Because classes being taught at the extension campuses required the use of computers, each of the extension facilities required a microcomputer LAN. NSU also provided a link between the file servers for these LAN's and NSU's academic computing center on the main campus.

NSU's rapid expansion placed a heavy load on the computing resources. The inability of the academic computing center to keep pace with the extra demands and new technologies precipitated the acquisition of computers by individual university departments. With these departmental acquisitions, the university's computing power increased significantly.

The General Events - Unification

In 1976, the state legislature began to take notice of the large sums of money being spent on higher education. The four independent state colleges, one of which was NSU, were sometimes expanding programs in the same areas. This resulted in considerable duplication of resources and expense. The state legislature, concerned about the inefficiency of redundant, costly programs, formed a higher education commission to study the issue. The outcome of the commission's study was to unify the four independent universities under one board of trustees. Rather than duplicating costly programs at each campus--for example, PhD. programs and colleges of medicine, engineering, and law--individual campuses were given a charter to become a primary provider of programs in certain areas. For example, one campus was designated the center for teacher education and fine arts, another the center for medicine and law, and so on. NSU was designated as the primary provider of agriculture, engineering, science, and business programs. Naturally, though each campus maintained a complete offering in the arts and sciences. As a result of this consolidation, the number of graduate programs, over all, was reduced by 50% and there was a 25% reduction in undergraduate programs.

Unification also carried consequences for the computing resources. NSU, for example, was chosen to house the state universities' scientific computer facility, though this facility is available to the other state universities as well.

The Specific Event - Technology Explosion

Because it offers PhD. degrees in engineering, computer sciences, and the natural sciences like chemistry, mathematics, and physics, NSU was always in the forefront of obtaining computing equipment. As mentioned earlier, NSU had allowed considerable autonomy to colleges and departments regarding what equipment was obtained and how it was installed and used. The only general university guidelines regarding computing equipment was that it be treated as a university resource. That is, all general purpose equipment could be used by faculty and students without regard to their department or major. The only exception to this policy was equipment that was obtained and used for specific purposes, for example, an engineering computer for robotics control was not available for student programming assignments. In contrast, a computer acquired to support FORTRAN programming classes for the engineering students was made equally available to students in other disciplines.

NSU's acquisition policy and the diverse needs of various departments, coupled with college and department rivalries, resulted in a large variety of computers being installed.

AN OVERVIEW OF NSU'S COMPUTING FACILITIES

Let's now look at some of the specifics regarding computing at NSU. The description does not include all resources; however, the major components are covered.

Administrative Computing

Administrative computing at NSU is separate from academic computing. The administrative computing center is located in the administration building and consists of the following computers and networking facilities.

- A mainframe computer for batch and on-line processing.
- A super-minicomputer network for office automation.
- A front-end processor to provide connection between administrative computing resources at NSU and other state universities.

. Terminals in all administrative offices and offices of the college deans.
. A variety of microcomputers.
. A data switch for incoming telephone lines.

The mainframe, an Amdahl computer, is used for most of the administrative computing functions, for example, student registration, student records, accounting, payroll, and so on. The office automation system, a network of Computer Consoles, Inc. computers, provides support for electronic mail, word processing, facsimile transfer, and document interchange.

The front-end processor (FEP), a Tandem NonStop system, controls all data communications with the mainframe and office automation systems. Since all data communication lines are controlled by the FEP, a user can connect to either of the two administrative systems. Moreover, the FEP can also provide a connection to other computing resources, for example, the administrative computers at the other state universities.

The microcomputers in the administrative area are a mixture of Apple Macintoshes and IBM compatibles. They function either as stand-alone systems or as terminals connected to the FEP. There is no local area network (LAN) connecting these systems. Through the host connections, the microcomputers are able to download data and word processing documents. The downloading facility is for disk-to-disk transfers. Microcomputer software, stored on one of the administrative systems can, therefore, be copied to a microcomputer's disk; however, microcomputer software on the hosts is not directly executable by a microcomputer. That is, the disks on the host do not function as virtual disks for the microcomputers. A schematic of the administrative computing system is given in Figure 2-1.

Academic Computing Center

The academic computing center is located in Science Hall. Science Hall was constructed in 1971 specifically to accommodate the expansion of the academic computer center. The principal academic computers are the scientific computer, a Control Data Corporation Cyber system, and a second Amdahl computer. The Amdahl is a mirror of the administrative system. Thus, the administrative and academic computing centers can back each other up should a major fault occur to one system. Access to the two academic systems is by terminals or by

Figure 2-1. Administrative Computing System

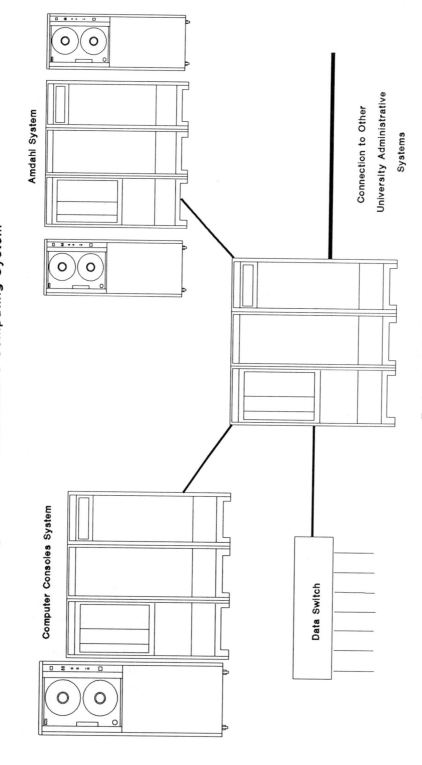

Amdahl System

Computer Consoles System

Tandem Front End Processor

Connection to Other University Administrative Systems

Data Switch

42

microcomputers using terminal emulation. The terminals and microcomputers are connected to a data switch that establishes connection to one of the academic machines based on the user's access request. Most terminals are located in the academic computer center, the library, student dormitories, and faculty offices. A few terminals are scattered among several other campus locations. Switched data communications access via the public telephone system is also provided.

The Amdahl system is a node on Internet, an international network consisting of nodes from universities and research corporations. Internet was formed by connecting several pre-existing networks, for example, connecting the ARPANET to NSFNET. Many of NSU's faculty regularly use Internet to communicate with researchers at other institutions and to obtain and disseminate information regarding research or teaching. Figure 2-2 depicts the academic computing center's systems.

The Computer Science Department

The Computer Science Department has a network of Digital Equipment Corporation (DEC) VAX systems. A Tandem NonStop system and a Sequent parallel processing system are available for courses in fault tolerant computing and parallel processing. Furthermore, the Computer Science Department has an Ethernet local area network (LAN) of microcomputer workstations. This LAN is connected to the VAX network. Several micro-VAXs provide file and print server functions for the LAN. The systems in the Computer Science Department are not connected to systems in the academic computing center or to computers in any other department. The Tandem and Sequent systems are accessible only through directly connected terminals or via switched access. Switched access to the VAX network is also provided. The Computer Science Department's computing configuration is shown in Figure 2-3.

The College of Engineering

The College of Engineering has the widest variety of equipment of all campus units. Some of this equipment is devoted to special purpose projects, for example, robotics and controlling or monitoring laboratory equipment. A description of the general purpose computing equipment follows.

The College of Engineering makes extensive use of the scientific computer and the Amdahl system in the academic computing center. These systems are used

Figure 2-2. Academic Computer Center

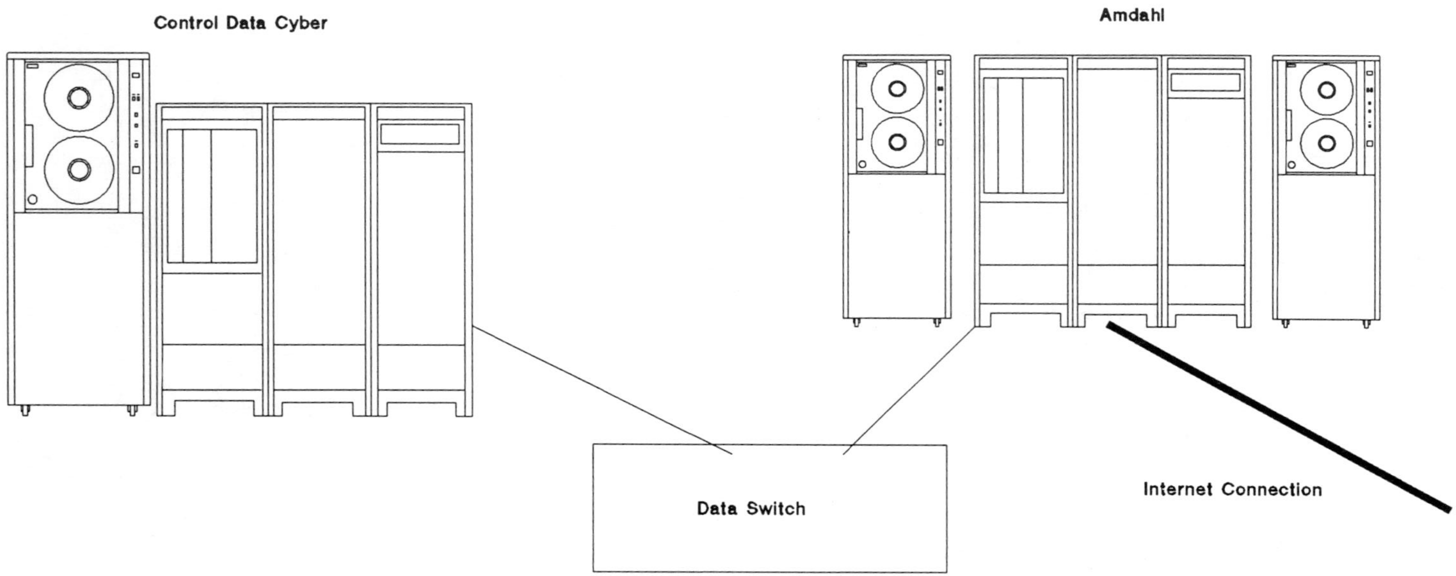

44

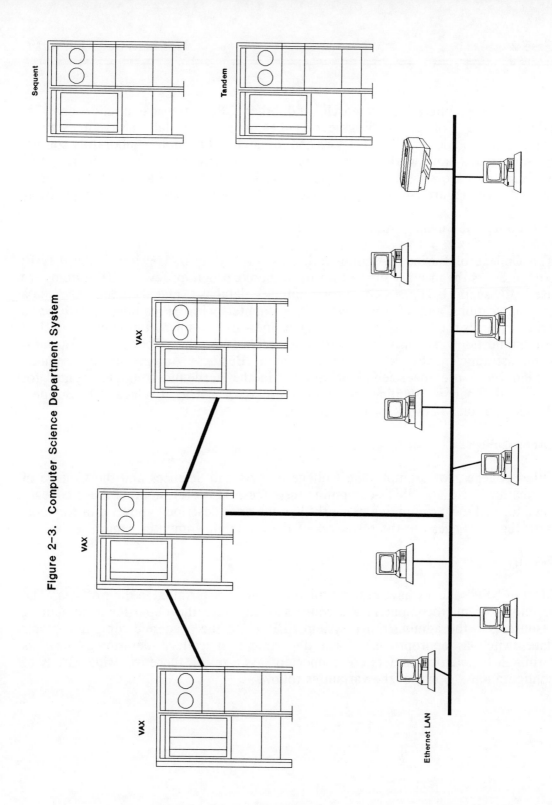

Figure 2-3. Computer Science Department System

for modelling, operations research, and other CPU intensive applications. In addition, the College of Engineering has a graphics laboratory to support computer-aided design (CAD) classes and research. The graphics laboratory consists of Sun Microsystem workstations connected to an Ethernet LAN. Several DEC VAX systems are also attached to this network, and switched access is provided to the network. Figure 2-4 shows the College of Engineering computing configuration.

The College of Business Administration

The College of Business Administration uses a variety of Hewlett Packard (HP) computers as the primary support for its academic program; several HP systems are used to support courses in programming, database management, and data communications, and a LAN of HP microcomputers with HP computers as file and print servers is used for courses teaching business uses of microcomputers. Switched communications is also provided for access to the College of Business Administration's network. Some College of Business Administration graduate students also use the scientific computer in the academic computer center for statistical analysis relating to their research. The College of Business Administration's network is shown in Figure 2-5.

Other Colleges

Other colleges, for example, the College of Arts and Sciences and the College of Agriculture, also use NSU's computing resources. However, none of these colleges have formed local computing networks like the ones described above. For the most part, these colleges use the resources of the academic computer center.

Faculty

Most of NSU's faculty have either a microcomputer or terminal in their offices. The terminals or microcomputers are connected either to the department computing resources, to the administrative system FEP, or to the academic computer center data switch as appropriate. Each department or college determines how its terminals or microcomputers are connected. As a result, there is a wide variety of configurations. Some of the variations follow.

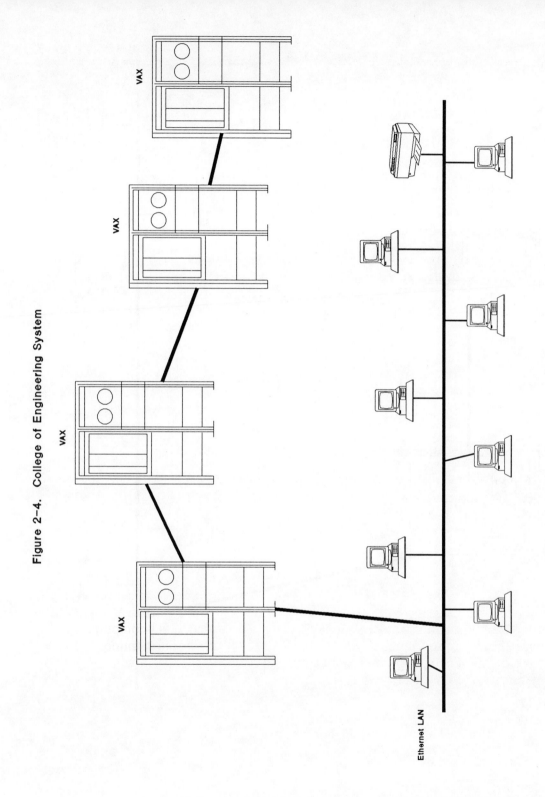

Figure 2-4. College of Engineering System

Figure 2-5. College of Business Administration System

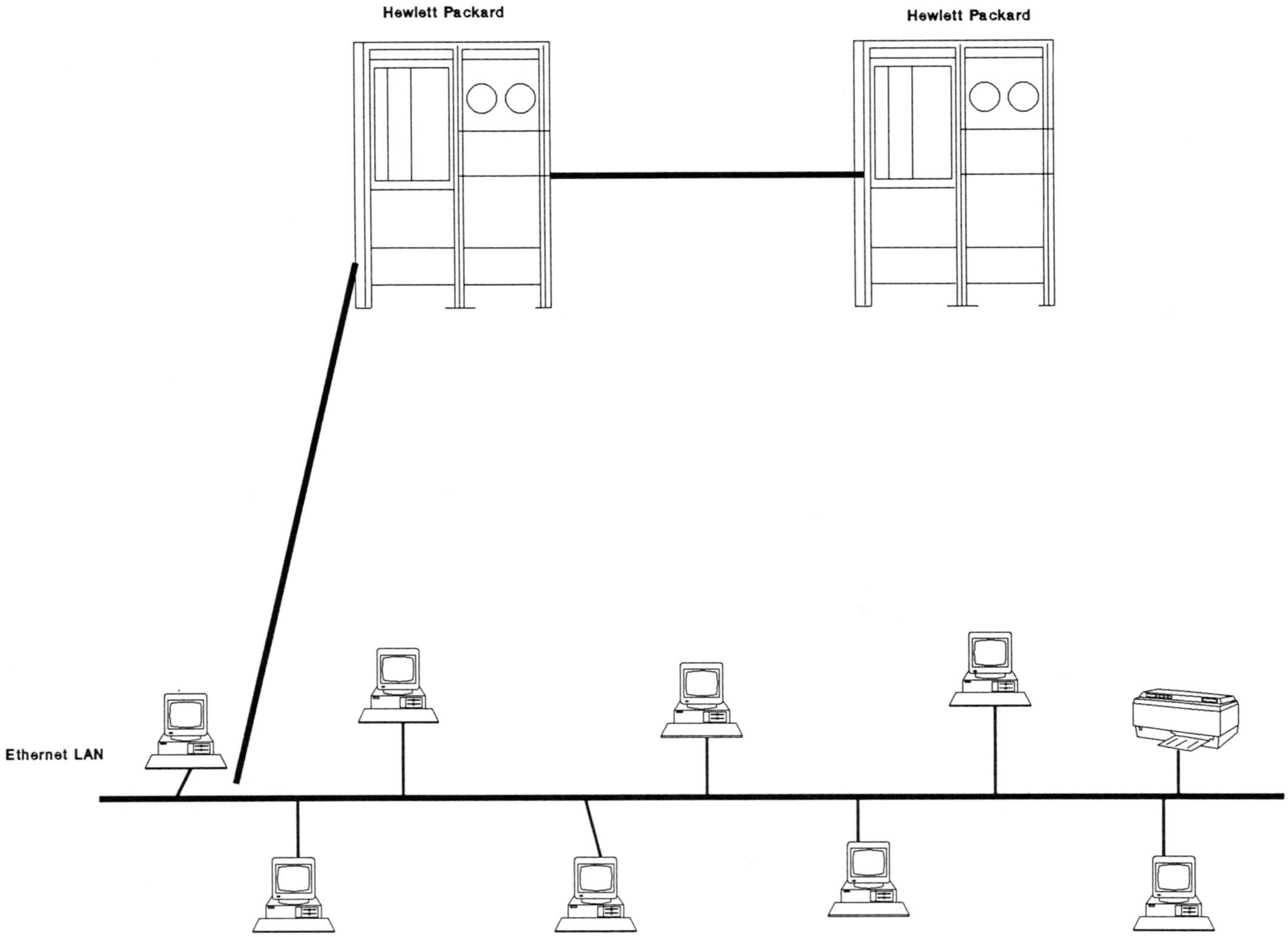

Hewlett Packard

Hewlett Packard

Ethernet LAN

In the College of Business Administration, each faculty member has an HP microcomputer that is attached to the College of Business Administration LAN. The Computer Science Department faculty also have microcomputers connected to their LAN. The English Department has a mixture of terminals and microcomputers to support its faculty; these are connected to the FEP on the administrative system because most of the faculty in the English Department use the word processing facilities of the office automation system for their writing. The College of Engineering's faculty use either terminals or microcomputers. The terminals are attached to the switch in the academic computing center or to the department's VAX network. All faculty microcomputers are attached to College of Engineering's LAN.

The most significant point of these connections is that a terminal or microcomputer has access to only one resource. For example, if a College of Engineering terminal is connected to the academic computer center, it cannot access the College of Engineering's VAX network. Microcomputers connected of the College of Business Administration's LAN cannot access the resources of the academic computing center.

Students

Students have a variety of ways for accessing NSU's academic computing facilities. Students do not have access to the administrative system. Access to LANs belonging to the various colleges and departments is via microcomputers in student laboratory rooms. College of Business Administration has three microcomputer laboratories, each of which has 30 workstations. The Computer Science Department has two microcomputer labs each of which has 32 workstations as well as a laboratory with terminals attached to the VAX network. The College of Engineering has a terminal room with 50 terminals attached to the academic computing center's data switch, a microcomputer laboratory with 40 microcomputers connected to the College of Engineering's LAN, and a graphics laboratory with 25 CAD workstations.

The academic computer center and the library each have terminal rooms. The terminals are attached to the data switch in the academic computing center, giving students access to either the Amdahl or the Cyber systems. Several of the dormitories also have microcomputer rooms; their microcomputers are attached to the data switch in the academic computing center.

Off-campus Facilities

NSU has three extension campuses. Each campus has a microcomputer laboratory where the microcomputers are connected by way of a LAN. Through a statistical multiplexer, the LAN file servers also provide the microcomputers with a connection to the data switch in the academic computing center. If necessary, the microcomputers in the off-campus laboratories can connect to the College of Business Administration HP computers or the Computer Science Department's and College of Engineering's VAX systems through switched communications links.

Other State Universities

The administrative and academic computing centers of the four state universities are linked together, allowing the universities to share software and files. The academic computing centers can also communicate with each other via the Internet network.

Networking

As noted earlier, NSU consists of islands of networks. The administrative system is networked with the administrative systems at the other three state universities; the academic system is a node on Internet and is connected to academic computer centers at the other state universities; the College of Business Administration, College of Engineering, and Computer Science Department each has a LAN consisting of microcomputers and larger systems. However, these islands of computing cannot effectively communicate with each other.

THE PROBLEM AT NSU

The computer facilities at NSU were acquired in bits and pieces on an as-needed basis. In the past, NSU had no long term plan for the acquisition and use of systems. The current situation evolved rather than resulting from planning. The only computer capabilities that were acquired and maintained on a university-wide basis are the academic and administrative systems.

The unmanaged proliferation of computing equipment is beginning to strain the financial resources of the university. The consolidation of the state universities has resulted in a smaller role and operating budget for each institution. At the direction of NSU's president, a university computer usage committee was formed to evaluate the current computer configurations and to make recommendations for both short-term and long-term directions. After six months of investigation and planning, the committee presented its report. The report cited four, somewhat related, major areas of concern--cost, management, unnecessary duplication of resources, and inability to share resources.

Cost

NSU's equipment acquisition represents nearly every possible way of obtaining equipment. Equipment has been purchased, leased, donated, and some is even on loan. All of it incurs costs of some sort. Naturally, the leased equipment has recurring monthly lease payments. All equipment also incurs one or more of the following costs.

- maintenance
- support
- back-up equipment
- telecommunications
- supplies
- software
- insurance
- security
- facilities

Maintenance. Most of the computers are covered under a hardware maintenance agreement with the vendor. The cost of maintenance varies from vendor to vendor, but averages approximately 1% of the equipment's purchase price per month. For the large computing systems, the monthly maintenance costs are in the tens of thousands of dollars.

NSU's academic computing center performs maintenance on many of the university's microcomputers and special purpose equipment. The costs for this are less than having the equipment covered by a third party maintenance agreement, but are still significant. Two full-time employees are budgeted for this purpose.

Moreover, the university keeps a modest inventory of spare equipment for replacing defective systems.

Support. For the larger systems--the Amdahl, Control Data, VAX, Tandem, and HP systems--NSU subscribes to the vendor's support agreements. This provides NSU with:

.   Vendor assistance in solving problems
.   Software upgrades
.   Manual updates

Although the cost of this service is much lower than the hardware maintenance agreements, it still represents a sizable annual expense.

Back-up equipment. As mentioned earlier, backup hardware is maintained for a variety of microcomputers. Spare equipment is also carried for some of the large system components, for example, printers, disk drives, memory, and so on. The diversity of equipment results in high levels of spares inventory, which consumes more of the university's money than would a standardized system.

Telecommunications. The local area networks all use media owned by NSU; however, there are a variety of data communications facilities leased from common carriers. All of the large system installations allow switched access, and approximately 100 telephone lines are available for this purpose. For example, the College of Business Administration's system has twelve available lines, the College of Engineering's system has sixteen, and the Computer Science Department's system has sixteen. During the peak usage times, the switched lines average 75% utilization, and therefore there is a campus-wide excess of at least 25 lines. Peaks occur at different times for each of the systems. For example, the peak use for administrative switched lines is at the beginning of each term during student registration. The academic system peaks usually occur at the end of the semester.

NSU also has a variety of leased telecommunications facilities. NSU is responsible for paying a share of the communications costs for the separate administrative and academic systems networks that tie the four state universities together. Attachment to Internet incurs a modest fee related to use of the network itself plus the cost of connection to the next closest Internet node. NSU is solely responsible for the cost of leased lines to each of the three campus extensions.

Supplies. Each facility stocks its own supplies--paper, printer ribbons, magnetic tapes, and so on. There is little sharing among units. Each unit naturally stocks sufficient supplies to avoid running out. The aggregate amount and cost of supplies is much larger than would be required if a central supply facility were used.

Software. Like supplies, each unit acquires the software it needs, and there is a reasonable amount of duplication in the software being used, but in several instances, NSU could have obtained a site license for software. The site licensing agreements would have allowed all NSU units use of that software. The cost of a site license is more than what an individual department paid, but less than the aggregate of the individual costs that NSU has incurred.

A hidden cost of each unit's ability to acquire its own software is the mixture of software being used. The computer usage committee observed that five different word processing packages were commonly used on the microcomputers alone. This lack of uniformity hid extra costs in training and software incompatibility.

Insurance. Almost all computing equipment is covered by insurance. The insurance costs are influenced by the environment in which the equipment is kept. For example, the administrative and academic computing centers receive reduced rates because these centers have fire suppression systems and are monitored by a closed circuit security system. The College of Business Administration system does not have these features and hence does not receive the discount.

Security. Some of the computing facilities have security devices. These include motion detectors, closed circuit television monitors, key card locks, and so on. The computer usage committee's report noted that cost savings will be realized if one or more facilities are combined. This will eliminate duplication of security capabilities and its associated costs.

Facilities. Like most of the costs just described, there is also duplication of facilities. These incur extra costs in terms of floor space, air conditioning, power, and so on.

Unnecessary Duplication of Resources

Unnecessary duplication of resources was cited several times earlier when describing the system costs. Duplication of resources is, in fact, the source of significant excess costs. In meeting its need for computing, each autonomous unit tended to size its facilities to meet peak demand. As a consequence, the aggregate of spare computing capacity throughout the campus is considerable. The resources that are duplicated include hardware, software, spare equipment, supplies, and personnel. The computer usage committee's report did not quantify the exact cost of this duplication, but suggested that annually it amounts to hundreds of thousands of dollars.

Computer Systems Operation and Management

Each of the computing facilities housing large systems requires an operations and management staff. Some of the staff are student employees, a few of whom qualify for work-study support. A portion of the salary for work-study students is paid from federal grants. Liberal use of student help reduces the operations and management support costs significantly.

Even though cost savings measures are used, the cost of people involved in system management at NSU is significant. Each of the College of Business Administration, College of Engineering, and Computer Science Department installations employ one full time operator/system manager. Each of these persons are supported by several student assistants and by the faculty. The academic and administrative computing centers have eight and ten full time operations employees. Student assistants and interns are also used in these centers to help with operations and programming. The administrative computing center has a director and two assistant directors. The academic computing center has a director and one assistant director. Both centers also employ a staff of application and system programmers. There are 27 full and part-time people at NSU employed in these capacities.

The academic computing center also has three full-time staff members whose job is to assist faculty and students with computer problems related to the academic computing facilities. The administrative computing center has two staff members who provide assistance and training for administrators and staff using that system.

Because the facilities are located in different buildings and because there is little sharing among the groups using the computer facilities, the number of people involved in system operations, management, programming, and support is greater than would be necessary if the facilities were consolidated.

Inability to Share Resources

The computer usage committee considered each of the preceding factors to be significant; however, the problem deemed most important by the committee is the inability of the different groups of computers and users to interface with each other.

Network Differences

As a result, if a College of Business Administration faculty member wants to send an electronic mail message to someone in the Computer Science department, he or she first needs to connect to the Computer Science system. The _easiest_ way to do this is to use a switched connection. This method is limiting because the speed of the link is 2400 bits per second (bps). Thus the _best_ method for making the connection is for the faculty member to go to the building housing the Computer Science Department and use one of the available terminals there. This provides a quality connection, one that is fast and reliable. Of course, this solution is inconvenient for the faculty member. Oddly, it is often more convenient for NSU's faculty to communicate with each other using Internet than via local facilities.

System Differences

Students are also inconvenienced by the independence of the systems. Even though it is possible for a student to write and test his or her computer science program on the College of Engineering's VAX system, it is difficult to port the program to the Computer Science system for electronic submission. Engineering students, many of whom take computer science classes, often find themselves moving from one computer facility to another to work on their assignments.

In addition to contending with different systems, students also have to cope with variations in microcomputer disk drives between the systems. Most of the Computer Science Department's microcomputers have 3-1/2 inch disk drives while those in the College of Engineering have 5-1/4 inch drives. A final difference exists in the login procedures, terminals, and text editors among the systems. Students using several different systems also must know how to use several text editors and hardware interfaces.

NSU's SHORT TERM COMPUTING OBJECTIVES

As mentioned earlier, the computer usage committee's report outlined problems, short term objectives, and long term goals. The short term objectives are as follows:

- Provide connection among all large systems, with the possible exception of the administrative computing system
- Provide a uniform campus-wide electronic mail system
- Provide campus-wide document and file exchange
- Allow all terminals and microcomputers currently attached to the existing systems to interface to all network nodes
- Control proliferation of computing equipment

Connecting the Large Systems

The key to all of the short term objectives is first consolidating all the large systems and the LANs into a common network. The only uncertainty in the computer usage committee's report regarding system interconnection is the administrative system. Having it available on the same network that students use poses security problems that the computer usage committee did not have the time to deal with. The computer usage committee recommended that additional analysis be done to determine if and how the administrative systems will be connected to the common network.

Technically, interconnection of NSU's subnets is easy; the difficult part is that concurrent with interconnection, the other short term objectives need to be satisfied. Some of the interconnection problems noted in the computer usage committee report were the following:

- Differing protocols
- Differing speeds
- Differing internal and network data formats

Differing protocols. Protocol differences exist at the data link, network, and transport layers. At the data link layer, the use of asynchronous protocols is widespread. Many of the terminals and microcomputers that are connected directly to a host system use an asynchronous protocol. The exception is some terminals connected to the Amdahl systems. Many of these connections use high-level data link control (HDLC) or binary synchronous protocols.

At the network and transport layers, there are also several network protocols being used. Each of the LANs use an IEEE 802.3 CSMA/CD bus architecture. The VAXs are connected using DECNET. An X.25 interface is used to connect to Internet. The network architecture used in the networks controlled by the Amdahl systems is essentially IBM's Systems Network Architecture (SNA).

Differing speeds. A variety of speeds are represented by the components that are to be linked together. The LANs operate at 10 Mbps while most of the short distance computer-to-computer links operate at 56 Kbps. Any networking solution will need to accommodate these speed differences.

Differing internal and network data formats. The internal data formats vary among the systems. Some systems use EBCDIC code while others use ASCII. Thus, transferring data from one node to another might require code conversion. Also, if an intermediate node, say an EBCDIC node, is needed as an intermediate node for communication between two ASCII nodes, then code conversion might have to occur twice.

The format for messages on the networks also varies among the systems. Presentation and session layer software will likely need to be written to accommodate these differences.

Electronic Mail System

At NSU, there are format differences among similar types of software that need to be accommodated. For example, four different electronic mail systems are in common use across campus. Either a mail interchange facility, say an X.400 facility, is needed, or a common mail system needs to be used. The computer usage committee believes that a campus-wide electronic mail system is an essential element of a network.

The computer usage committee considered the ideal solution to campus-wide mail to be for each unit to continue using the mail that they have become accustomed to and to build interfaces that will allow messages generated on one system to be acceptable to the mail system on any other node in the network.

Document and File Exchange

Campus-wide document exchange poses problems similar to mail exchange. The formats of documents, for example, word processing documents, graphics images, facsimile images, files, and so on, vary by machine. The objective of document transfer is to move the document from one network node to another and have it usable on the new node.

Document usability is just one of the problems needing a solution for document exchange. Another problem is the software essential for effecting the transfer. Software is necessary at the sending, intermediate, and receiving nodes to move a document from its source to its destination. At a minimum, the software will be responsible for flow control and error control. Other possible functions of this software might include data formatting, code conversion, and time staged delivery.

Connectivity of Current Equipment

The computer usage committee recommended that, where possible, the networking solution allow all terminals and microcomputers currently being used to interface to any system in the new network. Thus, microcomputers on College of Engineering's LAN ought also to function as SNA terminals and be involved in SNA sessions on the Amdahl. Likewise, terminals attached to the office automation system should have access to shared resources on any LAN.

Naturally, a terminal alone cannot download and run microcomputer software; however, microprocessor boards are available that can be connected to LAN servers or to a data switch. These boards provide a terminal with microcomputer-like capabilities. In essence, the terminal becomes the monitor and keyboard of the microcomputer board. To use this facility, the terminal should be connected to the microprocessor board. In this way, a terminal can also perform any of the functions of a microcomputer.

Control Equipment Proliferation

The computer usage committee was concerned about the proliferation of computing equipment. The number of systems at NSU had grown with no central planning and no unit coordination. Equipment had been acquired to fulfill specific needs, but without consideration for how it fit into the overall campus computing scheme. While the computer usage committee recognized that specialized equipment will always be necessary, the committee also recommended the implementation of measures for controlling equipment proliferation.

Personnel Control

The final short-term objective cited by the computer usage committee was to initiate a plan to make better use of computer operations, management, programming, and support personnel.

NSU's LONG TERM COMPUTING GOALS

The computer usage committee's long-term computing goals are oriented toward a permanent solution to the current problem together with procedures and policies that will prevent their recurrence. As an exercise, you will be asked to propose this solution.

YOU MAKE THE DECISIONS

Suppose that you were hired by NSU to help resolve their "islands of information" problem. Prepare a proposal for NSU's president consisting of solutions or suggestions for one or more of the following questions or exercises.

1. The computer usage committee indicated in its report that NSU's problem was unique to either their university or to universities in general. NSU's president wants to know if they are alone in this situation or if the problem has existed in other government or business sectors. Respond to the president's concern by providing details where companies in specific businesses or situations might experience similar

problems. If NSU is not unique in this regard, what steps did another organization take to solve this problem?

2. Suggest an approach for halting the proliferation of different kinds of computer equipment at NSU. Your suggestion should make use of existing equipment, reduce the variety of equipment procured, and make efficient use of personnel. Will your solution work for companies in general? Why or why not?

3. NSU has computer facilities in multiple locations and a variety of computer equipment. Discuss how this affects the need for personnel. You should address issues such as the number of support staff required, amount of training needed, and the ability of personnel to support more than one computing area. Suggest methods for improving this situation.

4. Design a network that will connect all of NSU's computing resources. Indicate how the interconnection is to be achieved. For example, show where bridges and gateways exist. List the functions each bridge and gateway must perform. Prepare a cost estimate for this network.

5. Suggest a solution for the mail and document/file transfer problem. Describe five functions your solution will need to address to be effective. Compare and contrast the two solutions suggested by the computer usage committee.

6. Are there some strategies NSU could use immediately to lower the costs of their operation? If so, describe them and indicate how they can be implemented.

7. Suppose you were a student at NSU. List three concerns you would have regarding the ease of use of the computing resources. Propose a solution for each of these problems.

8. Make a proposal for a long-term computing solution. Your proposal must abate the proliferation of equipment, reduce costs, reduce the number of personnel, and make all resources easily available to the user community. Moreover, the solution must continue to meet NSU's academic and administrative computing needs. Explain how each of the preceding points will be resolved by your proposal.

9. Propose details of a policy that will limit the proliferation of computer equipment at NSU. Make sure your proposal meets the needs of all user groups as well as the administration's needs for economy.

10. Propose details of a policy that will control the number of personnel hired in computer related jobs at NSU. Make sure your proposal meets the needs of all user groups as well as the administration's needs for economy.

THE ASSOCIATED BANKS

CASE OBJECTIVES

In this case several banks have been consolidated under a holding company. The holding company's objectives are to provide its customer base with consistent, comprehensive services. The key data communications factors to be considered in this case are:

- How to provide a short term solution to meet the bank's objectives for customer service and profitability.

- Which wide area network services to use.

- Which general implementation to choose-- centralized, decentralized, or distributed.

- If a decentralized or distributed option is chosen, should a homogeneous or heterogeneous environment be used.

- How to manage the option selected.

- How to provide security from fraud.

THE ASSOCIATED BANKS - AN OVERVIEW

The Associated Banks (TAB) was recently formed through the merger of eight independent regional banks in the western United States. TAB, the bank holding company, intends to further expand into the Midwest, Eastern Seaboard, and South to form a national bank chain. The first step in reaching this objective is to consolidate the initial eight banks and make them profitable.

The eight banks are located in the cities shown in Figure 3-1. Figure 3-2 shows the approximate air miles between TAB's member banks.

Figure 3-2. TAB Cities and the Approximate Air Mileage Between Them

	Alb	Boi	Den	Pho	Por	SLC	Sea	Tuc
Albuquerque, NM		940	437	458	1372	604	1453	568
Boise, ID	940		835	981	432	336	517	1091
Denver, CO	437	835		813	1261	534	1341	923
Phoenix, AZ	458	981	813		1268	645	1465	110
Portland, OR	1372	432	1261	1268		763	172	1371
Salt Lake Cty,UT	604	336	534	645	763		848	755
Seattle, WN	1453	517	1341	1465	172	848		1575
Tucson, AZ	568	1091	923	110	1371	755	1575	

BANK CONSOLIDATION

Consolidating the existing banks requires forming a management team to provide consistent direction, services, and marketing. The objectives of this effort are:

. To retain the individual character of each member bank.

. To allow a customer at any of the eight member banks to use the services of any other member bank.

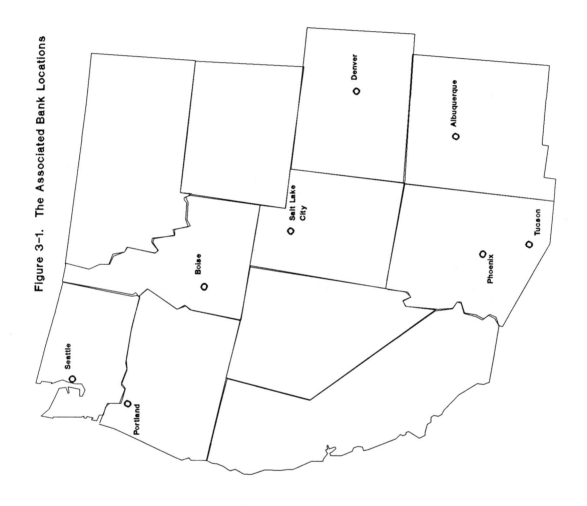

Figure 3-1. The Associated Bank Locations

. To make inter-bank transactions transparent to the bank's customers.

. To protect against fraud for inter-bank transactions.

. To provide uniform services at all banks.

. To be efficient and profitable.

A description of each of these objectives follows.

Maintain Bank Character

TAB anticipates that because of the consolidation, some of its customers will move their accounts. This conjecture is based on histories of other bank consolidations. Some customers prefer to bank with a local bank rather than with a regional or national chain of banks.

To minimize customer defections, TAB intends to maintain the individual character of each bank insofar as possible. Furthermore, if changes are deemed necessary, TAB intends to make them gradually. A wholesale set of changes at the outset is considered more likely to alienate customers than a gradual set of changes over time. Thus, commonly used instruments like deposit and withdrawal slips, check formats, and so on, will be retained at the outset. However, over time, TAB intends to standardize all such forms.

To further maintain each member bank's character, most of the bank's employees will be retained in their positions. The major personnel changes will occur at the bank's board level. A consolidated bank board will replace the boards of each of the member banks. For the most part, each bank will continue with its existing management structure of president, vice-presidents, and customer service personnel.

Interbank Services

Customers of each of the eight banks must be able to use the services of any of the other seven banks. The services include use of ATMs, check cashing privileges, savings account withdrawals, and so on. Each customer will have a "home" bank which is the bank at which their account is opened. For each customer, the other seven banks are termed "member" banks.

Even though a customer may have accounts at several TAB banks, the customer will always have only one home bank. For example, a corporation may have accounts at several banks; however, only one of the banks will be considered that corporation's home bank. The only exception to this will be a customer who opens several independent accounts; that is, when opening a second account at a member bank, the customer does not divulge an association with another TAB bank.

The concept of the home bank is to provide a focal point for banking services for each customer. For example, to provide consistent services for a corporate customer, that customer will be assigned a home bank and a home bank account representative. Typically, the home bank will be close to the customer's corporate or regional headquarters. The home bank account representative will be responsible for helping the customer attain consistent and proper service throughout all TAB member banks.

Transparent Transactions

When using the services of another member bank, customers must be able to perform transactions in essentially the same way they use the service at their home bank. A customer using the services of a member bank must be able to withdraw cash from a savings account in exactly the same way each member bank.

The only differences a customer might find in using member bank services is differences in forms such as deposit and withdrawal slips or differences in automated teller machines (ATMs). Most customers are already used to ATM differences.

Fraud Protection

In providing transparent access, TAB incurs a greater risk of fraud. When operating as individual banks, a teller processing a savings account or demand deposit account (checking account) withdrawal can check both the account balance and the customer's signature before effecting the withdrawal. At the outset of the consolidation, verifying the account balances and customer signatures between member banks will be difficult.

The technology for signature verification over communication links has been available for several years; however, since there are no communications links between member banks, there is no direct way for verifying account balances.

In the short term, the TAB banks must protect themselves against fraud in some other way. The following six measures are proposed.

. Disallow inter-bank transactions until a permanent solution is implemented.

. Phase implementation of inter-bank transactions by bringing member banks into a network two or three banks at a time.

. Use switched data communications links to verify balances.

. Use packet switching network services to provide member bank connections.

. Use voice communications to make authorizations.

. Trust the customers to do the right thing.

Disallow inter-bank transactions. A permanent solution to inter-bank transactions might take as long as a year to implement. In promoting the association of the banks, TAB touted the expanded customer service that would be available. Delaying inter-bank transactions is the most financially conservative of the six approaches but is also the least customer oriented.

Phased implementation. A phased implementation is a middle-of-the-road position. Linkage between a few member banks can be activated fairly quickly; a few might not be included for over a year. The pace at which the banks will be consolidated into one network depends on the software and hardware each is currently using. There is a considerable variety in the types of hardware and software among the member banks. These differences are described later.

Switched communications links. Switched communications links among the member banks can be used immediately as each bank already has switched connection capabilities. It is estimated that within a month a simple program can be designed, written, tested, and implemented to effect account balance inquiries, updates, and signature verification. It was noted that if the number of inter-bank transactions are many, this solution will result in frequent telephone calls and associated high telephone charges. A single withdrawal could easily cost the bank over a dollar in telephone charges. Moreover, the use of switched links poses a security problem. For example, they make TAB more vulnerable to hackers. A wide area telecommunications (WATS) service could be used to place a ceiling on telephone costs.

Packet switching. A packet switching network (PDN) solution is similar to the switched communications link solution. Several of the member banks are already subscribers to PDN services. TAB must determine which method is less expensive.

Voice authorizations. Voice authorizations are similar to switched communications facilities with the exception that verification is done by a teller rather than by computer-to-computer verification. This solution is possible as an immediate stop-gap measure pending installation of a long-term solution.

Trust customers. The final interim proposal is to trust customers to do the right thing. TAB knows that most customers do not overdraw their accounts, and that the majority of those who do, do so by mistake and replace the money and pay the associated penalties. Unfortunately, a few customers will discover that account balances are not being checked for inter-bank transactions and will exploit that weakness. Limiting the amounts of such transactions will help reduce the potential loss, but will not eliminate it altogether.

Obviously, each of these interim solutions have weaknesses. TAB needs to select one solution that will balance optimizing customer convenience while minimizing financial risks.

Providing Uniform Services

Providing uniform services somewhat contradicts the goal of maintaining each bank's individual character. A compromise between these two goals is obviously needed. Each member bank currently provides complete customer services. All have savings, demand deposit, and loan accounts, an ATM network, certificates of deposit, Visa and MasterCard credit or debit cards, Christmas Club accounts, travelers checks, lock boxes, and so on. Within these services, however, there is a variation among charges and conditions for the service. Some of these differences are:

- Types of demand deposit accounts. Some have minimum balances, pay interest, and are fee-free. Others have no minimum balance and incur monthly fees. There is a difference among the limits and fees charged.

- Some banks provide MasterCard or Visa cards as debit cards rather than credit cards. Several banks offer their customers an option of either debit or credit cards. Credit cards incur an annual fee, and the fee varies among the member banks. Debit cards have no annual fee.

- Interest rates for all types of accounts--savings, demand deposit, loan, and credit cards--vary among the member banks.

- Senior citizen and youth accounts are provided by six of the member banks. There are differences in the way these are implemented.

Besides the differences just cited, there are also some services that are offered by only one or a few banks. For example, three banks provide the ability to purchase stocks on the major stock exchanges through a discount brokerage house. One bank provides a financial counseling service. One bank is affiliated with a travel agency to provide those amenities to its customers.

TAB's ultimate goal is to have the same services at each bank and to have those services be consistent. That is, to charge the same rates and establish the same conditions for using each service.

Profitability and Efficiency

Above all, TAB must be profitable. The board anticipates that during the first year, profits may be low or the business may run at a loss; the costs of consolidation will likely erode profits at the outset. One of the keys to profitability is the ability to run an efficient operation, and a great deal of the efficiency will depend on how the bank computerizes its operations.

COMPUTING AT THE MEMBER BANKS

TAB management sees computerization as the key to consolidating the banks. Unfortunately, connecting the computing facilities of the member banks is not a simple task. Establishing the data communications links is, of course, easily accomplished. But establishing an environment where applications can communicate with each other is another issue. The problems arise because the hardware and software used by the member banks is not homogeneous. Thus, even though the computer systems can be easily networked, the software interfaces to allow immediate account inquiries and updates over the network are not in place. Let us now look at the basic systems being used at each member bank.

The Albuquerque Bank

The Albuquerque bank uses IBM hardware and a banking software system procured from a third party, Hogan Systems Incorporated. For on-line transactions, the software uses IBM's Customer Information Control System (CICS) as the transaction control process. For controlling ATM transactions, the Albuquerque bank uses Tandem Computers running Applied Communications Incorporated software.

The Boise Bank

The Boise bank is the smallest of the eight banks and one of two banks with unusual data processing procedures. Boise uses a service bureau to provide its computing services. The only in-house computers are five microcomputers. These are used for loan analysis and to locally process data downloaded from the service bureau. Boise owns the five microcomputers, the terminals that connect to the service bureau's system, and several ATMs. The service bureau also provides the ATM services for Boise.

The Denver Bank

The Denver bank uses Unisys hardware and software. For on-line processing, the transaction control process is a standard message control system offered by Unisys. The ATMs are also controlled by the Unisys system.

The Phoenix Bank

The Phoenix bank uses IBM hardware and software that was developed in-house. The on-line portion of the system runs under IBM's CICS transaction control process. The ATMs are also controlled by CICS.

The Portland Bank

The Portland bank uses basically the same hardware and software as the Denver bank.

The Salt Lake City Bank

The Salt Lake City bank uses Tandem hardware and Applied Communications Incorporated software. This software makes use of Tandem's PATHWAY transaction control process for on-line services.

The Seattle Bank

The Seattle bank uses the same system as both Denver and Portland.

The Tucson Bank

The Tucson bank has the second unique approach to computerized banking. In 1988, it decided to sell its aging mainframe system and replace it with a network of microcomputers and a file server on a local area network. The microcomputers are used to provide all on-line services including ATM, teller terminal, and loan analysis. A service bureau is used for batch processing--for example, check clearing.

Clearly, the banks have taken diverse courses in setting up computer services. With the exception of the banks using service bureaus, all of the banks own the equipment they use. The banks using a service bureau own all the equipment they use locally, that is, terminals, microcomputers, modems, and multiplexers.

TAB'S PRIMARY APPLICATIONS

TAB banks have a large number of applications. A brief description of the principal banking applications follows.

Automated Teller Machines

All banks own ATMs. The number of ATMs controlled by member banks varies from 12 to 74. All banks except one are also members of a regional or national ATM system that allows the bank's customers to use ATMs owned by another bank. The ATM services provided by each bank is similar; the differences are primarily in withdrawal limits and in the number and type of accounts that can be linked to the ATM service. ATMs on or near the bank's premises are directly connected to the bank's computer through a local controller. Remote ATMs are controlled by a concentrator. In consolidating the banks, TAB does not anticipate changing the existing ATM networks.

Teller Terminal

Teller terminal applications process all transactions submitted by tellers. This application typically provides the following functions.

- . Electronic journal.

- . Memo or on-line account posting.

- . Automatic balancing.

- . Off-line journal in case the host is unavailable, with the ability to post the updates when connection is re-established.

- . Enforcement of check cashing limits.

- . Security provisions.

- . Teller training modes.

Teller terminals in some banks are directly connected to the host processor. In other banks they are connected to a concentrator that communicates with the host processor. Use of a concentrator is always used for the banks that have branch banking offices.

Safe Deposit

The safe deposit application must track the customers subscribing to this service. Tracking includes generating bills when the lease expires, capturing the date, time, and name of the customer each time the box is used, maintaining an inventory of keys, recording payments received, printing tax deduction statements for box holders, bringing management attention to past due bills, and so on.

Loans

All member banks have software to assist with loan approval and processing. However, there is little consistency among these applications. TAB intends to have a standard loan application that also provides a loan officer with a certain amount of flexibility. The system will flag and automatically track loans made on an exception basis. Each loan officer will be given an exception limit. If a loan officer attempts to exceed this limit, a bank vice-president, who must not be the primary loan officer, must also approve the loan.

The loan application has several components as follows:

. Applicant information.

. Loan authorization.

. Loan pricing.

. Loan tracking.

Collections

The collections application is used to assist operators in collecting over-drafts, past-due loan payments, safe deposit renewal fees, and other receivables. The data that drives this application is supplied by the other application modules, for example, loans and safe deposit.

Funds Transfer

TAB banks all have the ability to transfer funds to and from other banks using a variety of methods. All use the Federal Reserve Bank's Fedwire funds transfer network. Most of the banks also use the SWIFT international funds transfer network. Other banks use the services of a correspondent bank for funds transfer. Under TAB, all banks will have each of these services available.

Point of Sale (POS)

Several of the member banks have implemented some version of POS applications. In POS, a merchant's electronic cash register is connected to the bank's network. A basic POS transaction authorizes a credit or debit card purchase. If the transaction involves a debit card, the amount of the purchase is transferred directly from the purchaser's account to the merchant's account if the purchaser is a customer at the bank.

TAB sees POS as a major profit service and wants each member bank to provide POS services to merchants. Moreover, it has plans for additional services in its POS applications. It will, of course, provide immediate debit card account updates for its customers and merchants regardless of the location in which the purchase is made. That is, if a customer having a home bank in Seattle uses his or her debit card at a store serviced by the Tucson bank, the Seattle customer's account will be immediately debited and the merchant's account will be credited with the purchase amount less the service charge.

Additional services that TAB wants to provide include the following:

. Check authorization.

. Electronic gas pumps.

. Inventory control.

. Merchant cash management.

. Electronic messages.

. Electronic draft capturing.

Check authorization. Electronic check authorization will be provided only for customers of a member bank. The customer benefits from the ease with which verification occurs, and the merchant benefits by having the check guaranteed by the bank.

Electronic gas pumps. The banks will control electronic gas pumps at subscriber stations. Customers will pay for the gas with a bank debit or credit card. The customer will insert the debit card into a card reader at the pump, and type in the amount of gas to be purchased. The computer controls the amount of gas pumped and immediately updates the accounts of both the customer and the station owner.

Inventory control. For small merchants that do not have computerized inventory systems, TAB will provide that service. As goods are purchased, the TAB system will update the store's inventory levels, generate re-stocking orders, and issue periodic inventory reports to the merchant.

Merchant cash management. TAB will also provide cash management services for merchants. With this service, TAB will move money between the accounts for a merchant to cover expenses while ensuring that the merchant's money is working at its maximum potential.

Electronic messages. For some merchants, electronic messages can assist in automating their business. For the electronic gas stations, price increases or decreases can be transmitted to each pump, and the price will be immediately and consistently changed at all or selected stations. For merchants subscribing to the inventory component of POS, price changes can also be made in the inventory database and those price changes will be immediately available at all of the merchant's POS terminals. Electronic messages will also be used to advise of stolen or misused credit cards.

Electronic draft capturing. TAB also intends to implement electronic draft capturing. This form of authorization eliminates the paper draft that has been historically used in processing a bank card transaction. With this service, TAB can lower the charges to merchants because these transactions can be processed more efficiently and because it reduces the float attributable to processing paper transactions.

If successfully implemented, the new POS services will not only attract new commercial customers, but will also be a significant new source of income.

Microcomputer Banking Services

TAB wants to be in a position to exploit the capabilities of its customer's home computers. None of the member banks currently offer such services. Some of the target services include cash management like that envisioned for merchants, bill payments, generation of statements on demand, and financial advisory services.

Management Information Support

TAB intends to make extensive use of information management tools to assist upper management in its decision making. None of the member banks currently have this capability. The type of decision support they desire will require an investment in fourth generation languages and expert systems. All member bank data must be available to these systems.

Security

Security is a primary concern for most banks. Some of the services TAB will provide--for example, microcomputer banking--provide potential for security abuses. With the microcomputer bill payment system, one user could potentially pay his or her bills from another person's account. Security measures need to be implemented to prevent such abuses.

IMPLEMENTATION APPROACHES

In computerizing its applications, TAB's options are essentially as follows:

. Centralized data processing.

. Decentralized data processing.

. Regional processing.

. Distributed data processing and databases.

Centralized Data Processing

A centralized approach to bank computerization will use one central data processing center. All member banks will use terminals or microcomputers to connect to the central facility, and all customer accounts and member bank databases will be maintained at the central facility. The only data maintained at individual member banks will be printed output and data that are extracted from the central database for local manipulation on microcomputers. A possible centralized configuration is represented by Figure 3-3.

Decentralized Data Processing

With decentralized data processing, each member bank will have its own computer system and customer database. Inquiries between banks can occur; however, the database is not truly distributed. For example, if a customer transfers money from one member bank to another, the transaction will not be able to span nodes as one

Figure 3-3. A Centralized Network Configuration

78

distributed transaction. Instead, the transfer will take place using the same facilities as funds transfers between banks that are not affiliated.

Using a decentralized solution, each member bank is responsible for its own operations and applications. The only responsibility one member bank has to other member banks is to provide the interfaces that allow account inquiries and updates. Otherwise, each bank is relatively free to select its own hardware and software and to manage its system as it sees fit. A possible decentralized configuration is shown in Figure 3-4.

Regional Processing Centers

Establishing regional processing centers is a compromise between a centralized system and a completely decentralized system. With regional processing, TAB will establish two or more processing centers, each of which will provide processing support for two or more member banks. All regional centers will be networked to provide complete inter-bank linkages. A sample configuration of this implementation is shown in Figure 3-5.

Distributed Data Processing/Databases

With a distributed database, TAB has the advantages of both a centralized and distributed system. Data will be distributed and located closest to where it is used. The distributed database will make the data distribution transparent to the users of the system. Thus, information can be retrieved from multiple nodes as though it were located on one centralized node. A distributed network configuration will look much like the decentralized configuration shown in Figure 3-4. The difference between the two will be primarily in the software implementation.

YOU MAKE THE DECISIONS

Assume that you have been retained by TAB to assist in designing the banking network. TAB has suggested the implementations presented earlier as likely alternatives, but you are not constrained by these suggestions. Some of the information TAB needs to reach a decision will result from the following questions and exercises.

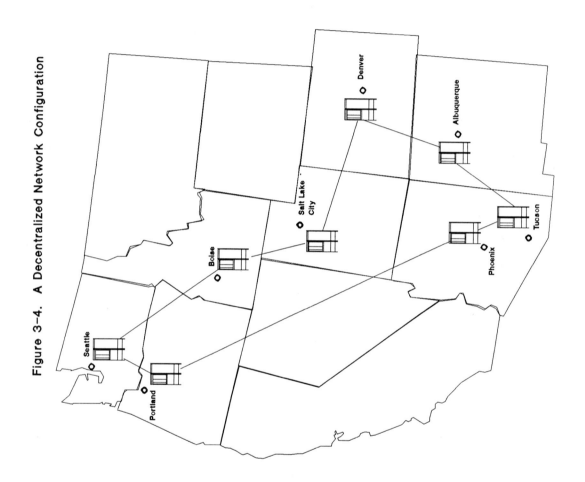

Figure 3-4. A Decentralized Network Configuration

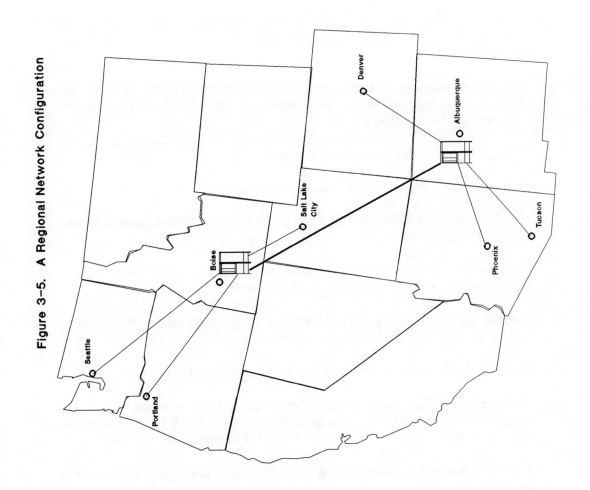

Figure 3–5. A Regional Network Configuration

1. Rank the interim solutions to inter-bank communications in order by security. Place the most secure solution first and the least secure system last. Explain your ranking.

2. Rank the interim solutions to inter-bank communications in order of their ease of implementation. Place the easiest implementation first and the most difficult last. Explain your ranking.

3. Rank the interim solutions to inter-bank communications in order of their cost. Place the least expensive first and the most expensive last. For making your cost estimates, use the following information.

- Mileage between cities as given in Figure 3-2.

- Determine and use the minimum distance network.

- Use fault-tolerant links; that is, each node must be linked to at least two different neighbors.

- Use the cost figures in the Appendix A or obtain current cost figures. Document the source of figures used in your calculations.

- Assume each bank will generate 500 inquiries to other banks. The queries will be equally divided among all member banks.

- Each bank will receive 500 inquiries from other banks.

- All transactions are equally spaced over an eight hour work day. Each requires four transmissions, two in each direction. Each transmission will consist of 100 characters of data and control information.

- Use 9600 bps and 2400 bps line speeds for leased lines and switched lines respectively.

- Make and document any additional assumptions you make in preparing the cost estimates.

4. Explain the advantages and disadvantages of a centralized system.

5. Explain the advantages and disadvantages of a decentralized system.

6. Explain the advantages and disadvantages of regional processing centers.

7. Explain the advantages and disadvantages of a distributed system.

8. Would you propose that TAB consider a fifth alternative to those of questions 4 through 7? If so, what alternative(s) should they consider? What are the advantages and disadvantages of this solution(s)?

9. Rank each of the alternatives of exercises 4 through 8 in terms of:
    a. new equipment or transmission facilities required
    b. effective use of existing equipment

Explain your rankings and describe the new equipment or transmission facilities required.

10. Which of the alternatives in exercises 4 through 8 will be the easiest to manage? Which will be the most difficult to manage? Explain your answer in detail.

11. Which of the alternatives in exercises 4 through 8 will be the most reliable? Explain your answer in detail.

12. How can the transaction control processes assist in providing transparent access for a decentralized, regionalized, or distributed system? That is, how can a transaction control process assist in accepting and responding to messages from other banks?

13. Make a recommendation to TAB for an interim solution to bank interconnection. Justify your recommendation.

14. Recommend a long term computer solution to TAB. Justify your recommendation by showing how it is superior to other alternatives.

15. Diagram the network you recommended in exercise 14. Show all processing nodes and communications links.

16. Define four security measures that TAB should implement. Describe how these measures will reduce the chance of fraud.

17. TAB has some applications that can be easily centralized, for example, payroll. How do you recommend that such applications be implemented for each of the following kinds of networks?
        a) decentralized
        b) distributed
        c) regional

FINANCIAL CONSULTANTS INTERNATIONAL

CASE OBJECTIVES

This case focuses primarily on two issues, international networks and network management. In the case exercises, you will need to evaluate the following:

. Problems that may exist in establishing data communications links that cross national borders.

. Problems inherent in managing a network that spans time zones, languages, cultures, and national regulations.

. Problems inherent in managing a network of diverse hardware and software.

. Differences between centralized network control and decentralized network control.

. Problems inherent in resolving problems that involve distant locations and more than one provider of hardware, software, or data communications facilities.

FINANCIAL CONSULTANTS INTERNATIONAL - AN OVERVIEW

Financial Consultants International (FCI) has just been formed through a consolidation of three financial consulting companies. Of the three companies, one operates in Europe, one in North America, and one in the Pacific Basin.

Each of the three original consulting companies is computerized; however, each company varies in their approach to using computers. FCI intends to provide common computing services to all offices. To make these services available, FCI will establish a global computer network linking all offices. To understand the complexity of this undertaking, let's now look at the computing facilities of the three original companies.

FCI'S EUROPEAN COMPUTING FACILITIES

The European group has offices in London, Paris, Rome, Frankfurt, Munich, Geneva, Zurich, Madrid, and Copenhagen, and most of these cities have several offices. All offices have computers, but there is no standard configuration or manufacturer. In each city there is a main office called the central office; the other offices are called satellite offices. Central offices each have a large mainframe that houses the main financial database for that country. Satellite offices have a mixture of minicomputers and microcomputers, all of which have access to the central office's mainframe. Examples of connections between satellite and central offices are shown in Figure 4-1 and 4-2.

Computers used in the European offices are made by a variety of vendors. As might be expected, the majority are manufactured by European companies. Usually, the computers used in a country are manufactured in that country.

Networks exist within individual countries, but there is no network that crosses an international border. For example, the Munich and Frankfurt central office mainframes are networked. Satellite offices in each of those cities are connected only to that city's central office; however, through the central office network, satellite offices in Munich can communicate with satellite offices in Frankfurt. The same is true in other countries. That is, each satellite office in a country can communicate with all other satellite and central offices in that country. Many offices also have local area networks (LAN) connecting the processors in the office.

Most often an FCI client seeks financial advice regarding their country of residence. That is, a client seeking advice in Rome most often is interested in Italian investments. Occasionally, however, an Italian client may need financial advice for another country, for example, France. On these occasions, the client is placed in personal contact with the French office. Thus, computer connections between two countries are not necessary.

Figure 4-1. Single Central Office Configuration

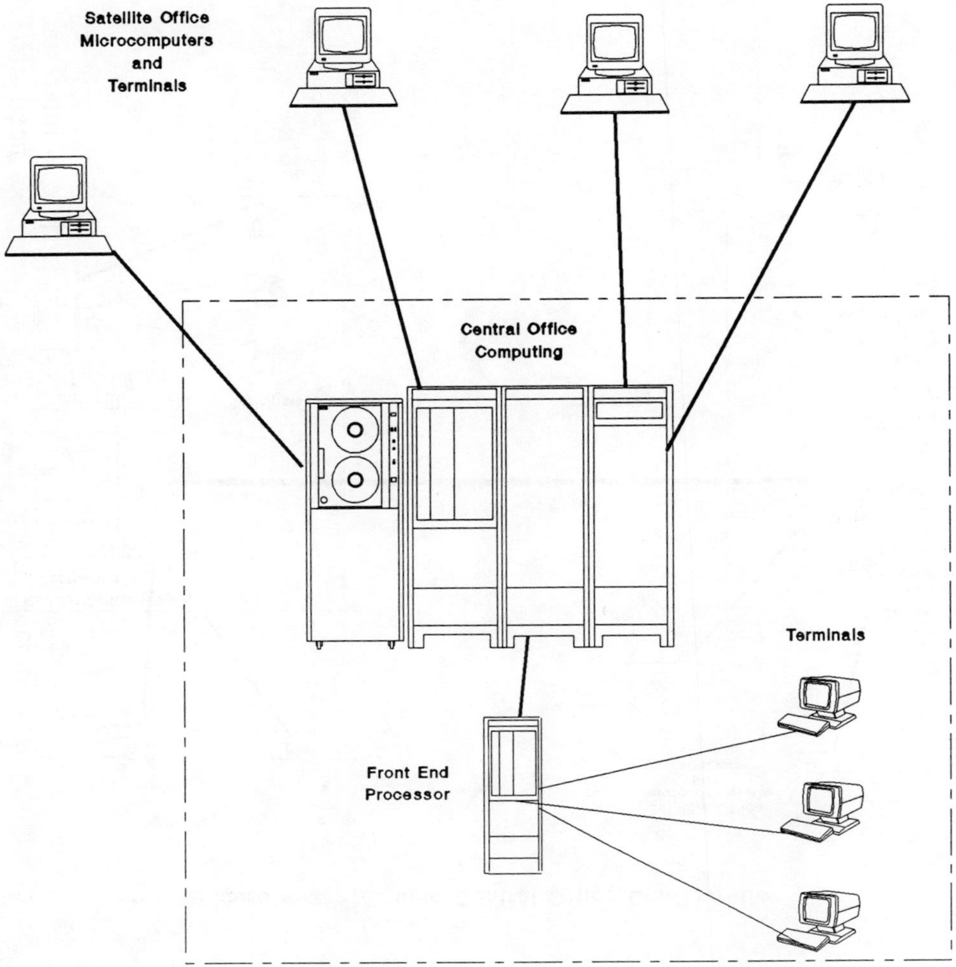

Satellite Office
Microcomputers
and
Terminals

Central Office
Computing

Front End
Processor

Terminals

87

Figure 4-2. Multiple Central Office Configuration

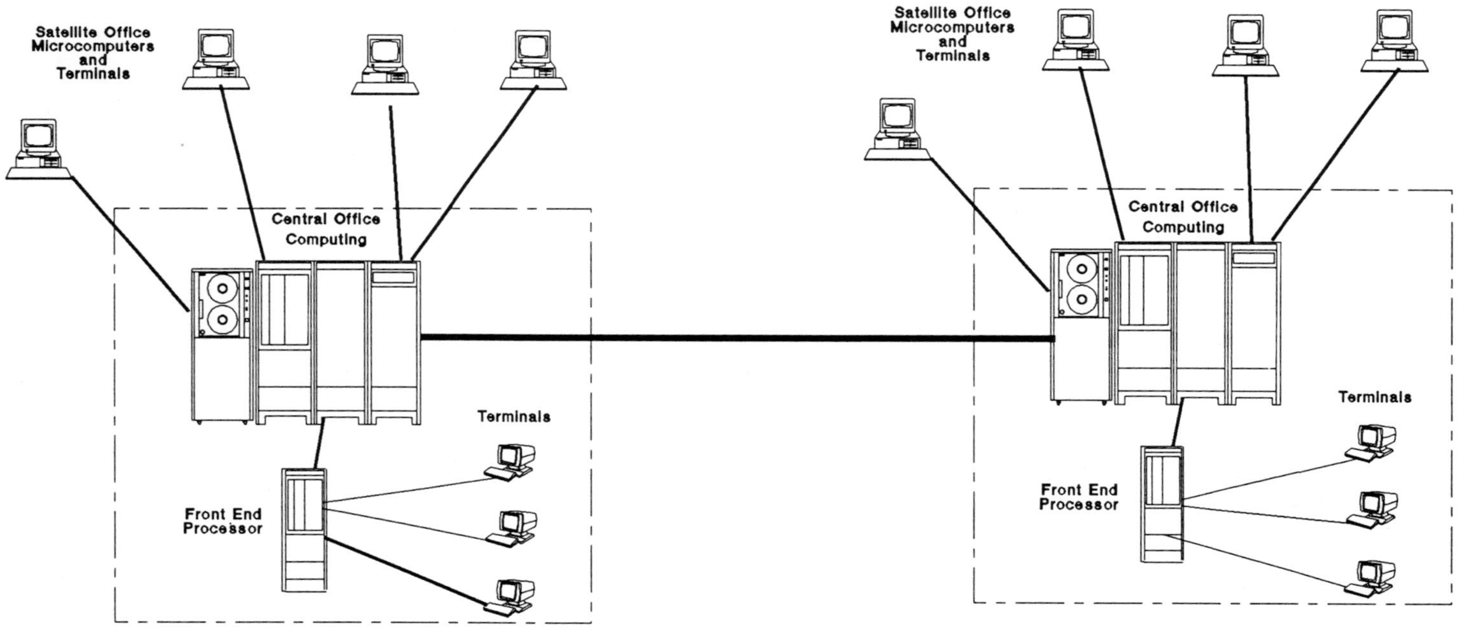

FCI's European offices have found that it takes more than computer databases to provide sound financial advice. A knowledge of the business practices and regulations in each country are also important. Thus, the consultants in one country rarely provide financial advice for another country. This is another reason for not networking the computers and databases between countries.

Establishing networks across national boundaries has not been essential for the manner in which FCI conducts business. There are two additional reasons that dissuaded FCI from establishing a European network. The first of these was the complexity of obtaining services between international locations. When many of FCI's offices started using computers, establishing a network involving communications providers from two different countries was sometimes difficult. Although today this is much easier, FCI has stuck with its earlier decision to establish networks only within a country.

A final reason for not establishing networks across country boundaries has to do with national legislation. Some countries consider some of the data held in FCI's databases to be sensitive. These countries attempt to restrict the dissemination of this data. In attempting to avoid close scrutiny of their operations, FCI elected to avoid international networking.

The European computing configuration is shown in Figure 4-3.

FCI'S PACIFIC BASIN COMPUTING FACILITIES

Computerization in the Pacific Basin is similar to that of Europe. FCI has offices in Tokyo, Osaka, Seoul, Taipei, Hong Kong, Singapore, Sydney, Melbourne, Perth, and Auckland. Central and satellite offices in each country are networked; however, there is only one international network, one connecting New Zealand and Australian offices.

The Pacific Basin computing facilities are shown in Figure 4-4.

FCI'S NORTH AMERICAN COMPUTING FACILITIES

The North American group has offices in Montreal, Toronto, Vancouver, New York, Chicago, San Francisco, Los Angeles, Houston, and Miami. All of these cities are

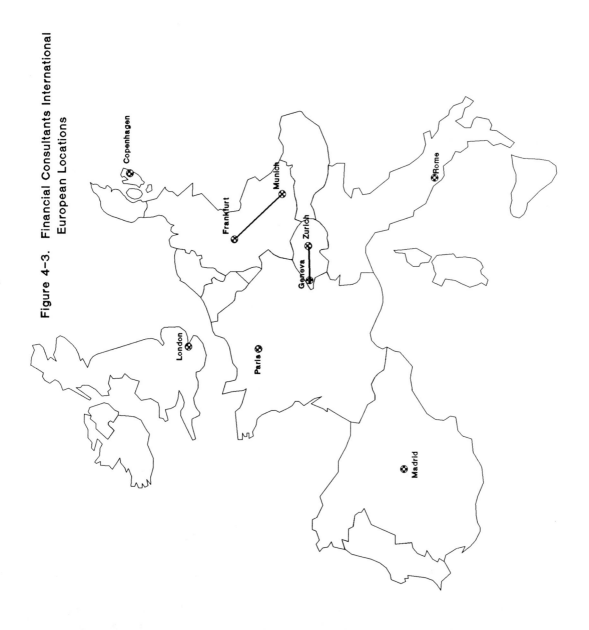

Figure 4-3. Financial Consultants International European Locations

Figure 4-4. Financial Consultants International Pacific Rim Computing

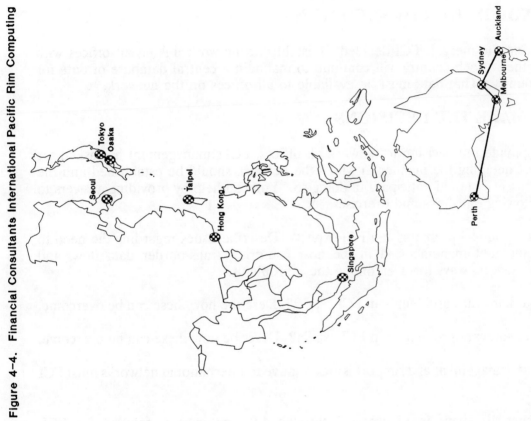

connected by a network. Two central databases are maintained, one in New York for U.S. data and one in Montreal for Canadian data. Data flows freely between cities without regard for national borders.

The North American network is shown in Figure 4-5.

CONSOLIDATION OF FACILITIES

Following the merger, FCI decided to establish a network linking all offices with each other. Each country will continue to maintain a central database of data for that country. That data must be available to all offices on the network.

YOU MAKE THE DECISIONS

Having made the decision to network all offices, FCI's management has asked for a report detailing the manner in which the network should be established and the problems FCI should anticipate in doing so. You can help by providing answers to the following questions and exercises.

1. What political problems can FCI expect? Describe issues regarding the need to use equipment manufactured in the host countries, trans-border data flow, and tariffs. Suggest ways for overcoming these problems.

2. What hardware problems can FCI expect? Describe how these can be overcome.

3. What software problems can FCI expect? Describe how these can be overcome.

4. What management and support issues relative to international networks must FCI resolve?

5. Using the maps in Figures 4-6 through 4-9, configure a network for FCI. Describe the types of links used to connect the three regions. That is, what type of transmission facilities do you recommend? Explain your choice. What parameters influenced your choice? What changes in these parameters would lead to a different choice?

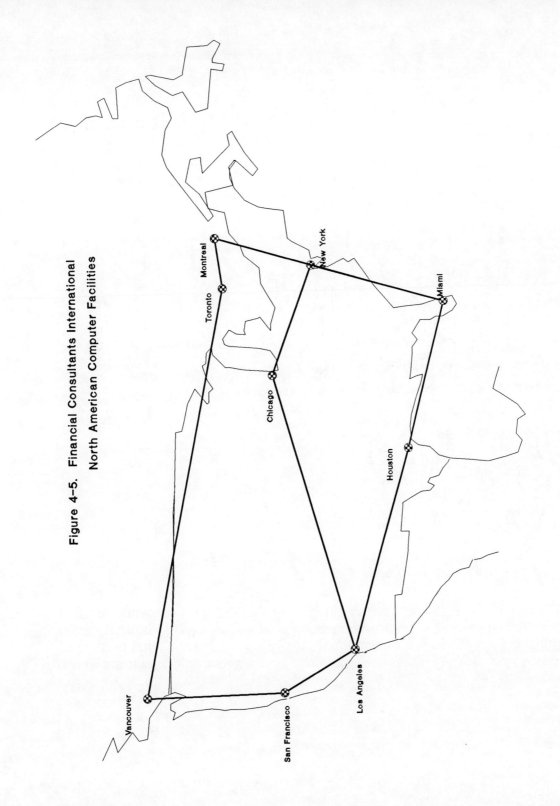

Figure 4–5. Financial Consultants International
North American Computer Facilities

93

Figure 4-6. Financial Consultants International European Locations

Copenhagen

Munich

Frankfurt

Zurich

Geneva

Rome

London

Paris

Madrid

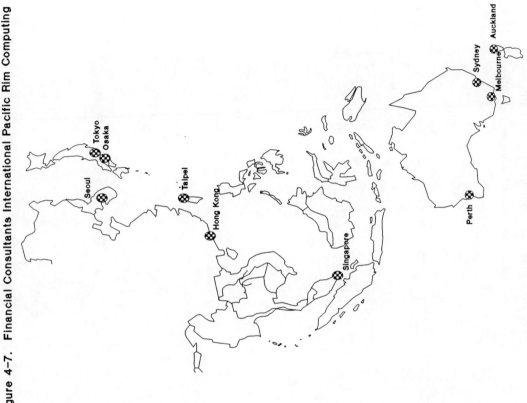

Figure 4-7. Financial Consultants International Pacific Rim Computing

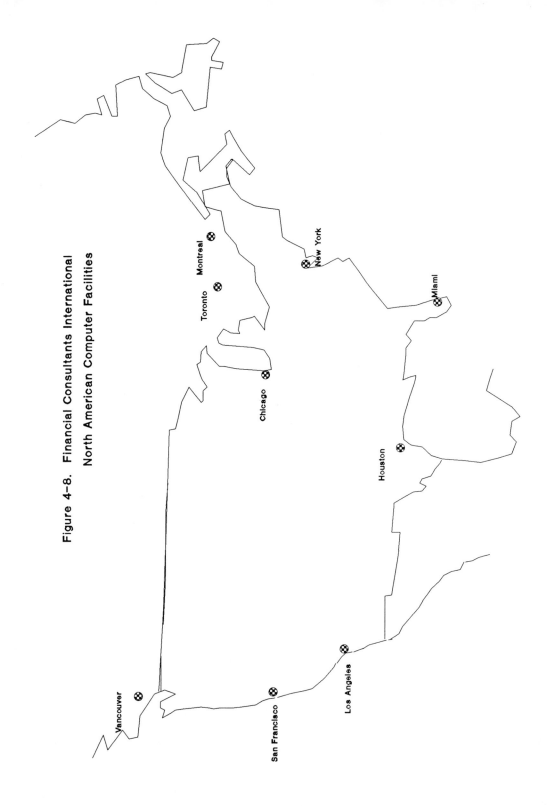

Figure 4-8. Financial Consultants International North American Computer Facilities

Figure 4-9. Financial Consultants International Cities

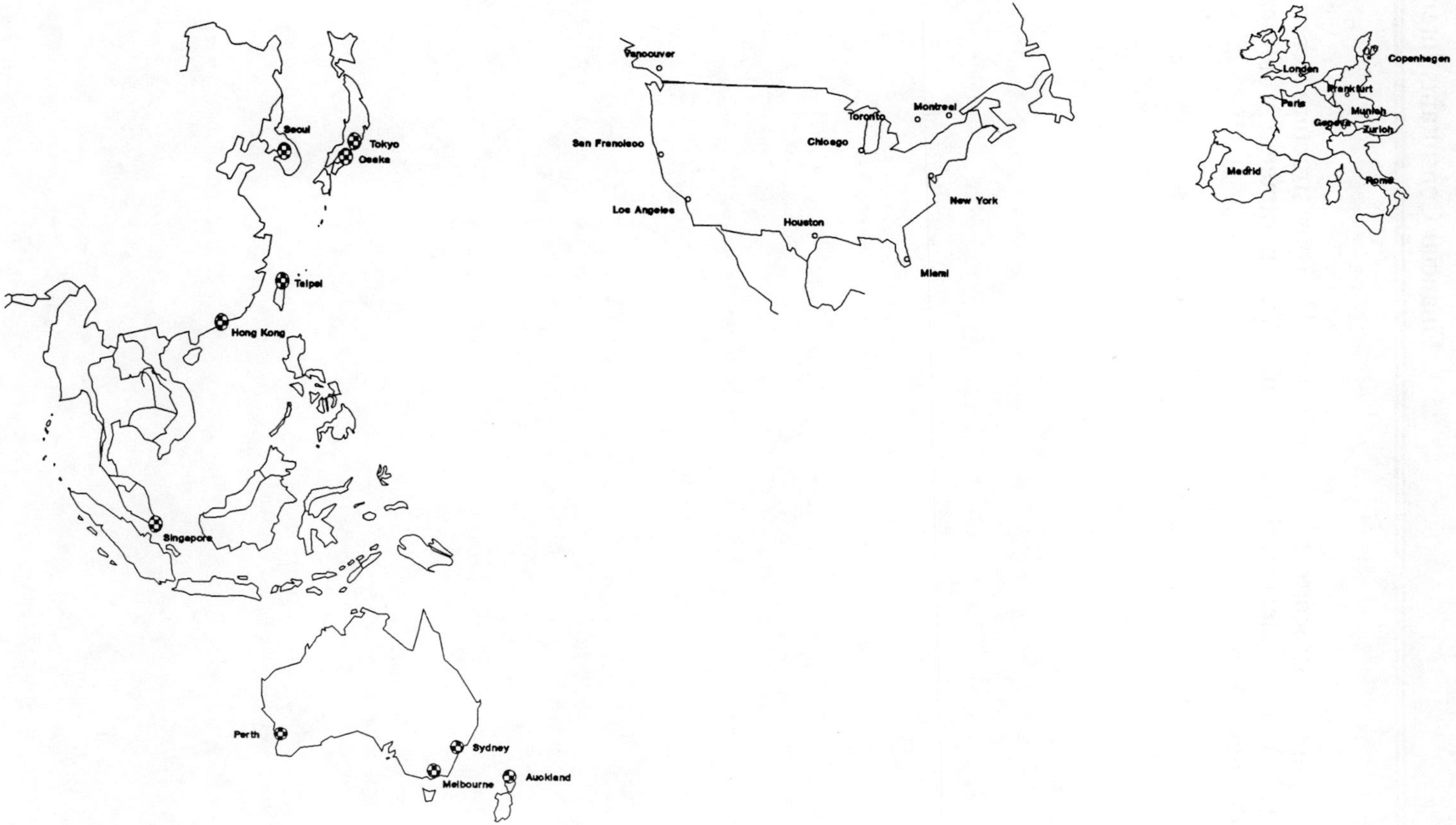

6. Define a support structure for the network. Is your structure centralized or decentralized? What influenced this decision? What parameters would cause you to change this decision?

Archer Freight Lines

CASE OBJECTIVE

Microcomputers have become a significant force in computer networks. Most users are already familiar with the role microcomputers play in local area networks (LAN). The first case study, the Balboa Insurance Agency, addresses the role of microcomputers and LANs in a small office setting, and Case 2, Northern State University, discusses the use of larger LANs. This case looks at a different application of microcomputers, specifically, how they can be used in a more traditional computer network, one with a large host processing system. In this case you will analyze how to use microcomputers in this more traditional processing environment. The topics covered in this case include:

- . Micro-to-mainframe links.

- . Microcomputer data communications software for micro-to-mainframe links.

- . Mainframe data communications software for micro-to-mainframe links.

- . Microcomputer data communications hardware for micro-to-mainframe links.

ARCHER FREIGHT LINES - AN OVERVIEW

Archer Freight Lines (AFL) is a regional truck freight company. AFL's primary area of operation is the American Midwest. It has freight offices in 50 towns and cities in this area. The company has experienced rapid growth over the last five years. Two effects of this growth have been the erosion of AFL's cash position due to financing its expansion and a growing strain on the capacity of the computing system.

The Cost of Expansion

To accommodate the company's growth, management has invested heavily in equipment, tractors and trailers, as well as in offices and maintenance facilities. Although the company is profitable, its cash flow is currently a major management concern, particularly because economists have predicted a general economic downturn for the region serviced by AFL. As a result, AFL's management has curtailed large capital expenditures.

AFL's expansion has also affected computer usage. Three times over the last five years, the hardware system has been upgraded with additional memory, data communications lines, disk drives, and so on. With the last expansion, the system reached its expansion limits. This means that additional computing resources cannot be added to the system. Expanding AFL's computing capabilities will thus require a new, larger computer or additional computers. Meanwhile, the processing demands are continuing to increase as AFL assumes new business and implements new applications.

Effective use of computers has been one of the contributors to AFL's success. The company has several new applications being designed to further extend its competitive edge. Since the current system cannot be expanded further, AFL will need to upgrade to a larger system. Upgrading to a larger system will incur one of those large expenses AFL is trying to avoid. Preliminary estimates for the cost of a computer upgrade exceed $500,000 for the hardware alone. A detailed estimate for a computer upgrade has not been done; however, AFL's management is positive that the $500,000 figure is optimistic; that is, management believes that the total cost will be higher.

As a result of this dilemma between needing more computer resources and lower corporate spending, AFL has decided to search for relatively low cost ways to increase computing power. One alternative being considered is the use of microcomputers. Before exploring this alternative, let us first look at the current state of computing at AFL.

AFL's Current Computing System

AFL started its computer operations in 1968 with a relatively small mainframe computer. As the business grew, AFL was usually able to upgrade the system in modest increments to keep pace with the company's growth. On three occasions, however, the upgrade was to a larger system. AFL's current system is a late model computer with over 125 terminals connected. These terminals are located in AFL's home office, fleet maintenance shops, and remote freight offices.

At the peak processing load, the number of active terminals is approximately 70. The peak processing load stresses the limits of the system, particularly when using CPU bound scheduling and routing applications. During these periods, users have begun experiencing abnormally long response times. As the new applications are brought on-line, computer usage is expected to increase even more, and the already slow response times will deteriorate even further.

Commonly used applications at AFL fall into six general categories: office administration, accounting and financial, management information, scheduling and routing, fleet maintenance, and customer service. Regardless of the type of application being used, the interface to the system is through a variety of terminals.

Home Office Computing

AFL uses a variety of terminals because the terminals have been acquired over time as the company grew. Some are dumb asynchronous hard copy and CRT terminals that were acquired with the original system in 1968. All of the newer terminals are smart terminals operating in synchronous or asynchronous mode. In general, new equipment has been installed in the home office, and the older equipment has been moved to the remote offices. Terminals in the home office are connected directly to the computer, and, for the most part, operate at speeds of either 9600 bits per second (bps) or 19,200 bps. Home office users have a wider range of applications available than remote users.

Remote Office Computing

Remote users are restricted in the applications they can use by lower line speeds (either 1200 or 2400 bps), the cost of transmission facilities, and in many cases, by slow, hard copy terminals. Over the past year, personnel in the remote offices have requested additional computer support. The type of processing support they are looking for includes word processing, database applications, scheduling, accounting, and spreadsheet analysis.

Expansion of computing capabilities at the remote offices using AFL's existing technology will also increase AFL's data communications costs. Currently, the messages exchanged between a terminal and its host are relatively small. However, most of AFL's new applications require page mode terminal capabilities and will not run on many of the remote terminals. Using these applications remotely will significantly increase the message traffic. The use of microcomputers will possibly allow some of the needed work to be done locally and reduce this anticipated additional cost.

ANALYSIS OF AFL's TERMINAL NETWORK

At AFL, microcomputers can be used effectively in place of terminals; however, replacement of every terminal with a microcomputer will be nearly as expensive as a computer upgrade. AFL has determined that microcomputers equipped to its needs will cost approximately $5,000 each. Recall that there are nearly 125 terminals being used within the company. A strategic replacement program, however, may be able to realize the goal of providing computational power where needed at reduced data communications costs and without increasing the load on the host system.

Annette Palmisano, one of AFL's systems analysts, has been given the project of analyzing the existing system, determining how microcomputers might be used within it, and recommending one or more solutions. Palmisano's report is divided into three sections--details of the existing terminal network, ways in which microcomputers can be linked to a host system, and recommended approaches. Details of the first two parts are given in the following sections. Some of the information in the report duplicates information provided earlier in the overview of AFL's system.

Part 1. Terminal Distribution and Connection

Terminals at AFL are installed in all company locations--home office, maintenance ships, and remote offices. In some locations, the environment dictates the type of terminal being used. For example, terminals in the fleet maintenance shops are specially constructed for operation in a hostile environment--an environment with wide temperature fluctuations and dirty air.

Most of the remote freight office terminals are connected via an X.25 link. This method of connection was used because the number of messages between a freight office and the home office is small, but connection must be established throughout the work day. In AFL's first years of operation the message traffic was insufficient for leased lines, and individual telephone calls would have been more expensive than the X.25 service.

Typically, a freight office contacts the home office each morning and evening to report equipment status and to obtain shipping schedules and routes. During the day, an office will connect to the computer to perform tasks such as tracking shipments, making shipment updates, or sending or receiving electronic mail. Most of these terminals are the old, hard copy devices. Several of the larger freight offices have several terminals, but most of the freight offices have only one.

Terminal Types by Location

A breakdown of the number of terminals and their locations is given in Figure 5-1. A narrative description of the terminal distribution follows.

The company has 122 terminals in use. The home office has 35 terminals, most of which are smart terminals that are typically operated in page mode; that is, the terminals are used for applications that make use of the entire screen. Of the eight dumb home office CRT terminals, three are used as consoles in the computer room. The remaining five dumb CRTs are used by the programming staff for system testing and text editing. The two hard copy terminals are used as computer room terminals to log system messages and for operations that require a hard copy log of the activity, for example, database recovery operations.

AFL has three maintenance shops, one of which is in the same building complex as the home office. Each maintenance facility has five terminals. The

Figure 5-1. Distribution of Terminals By Location

Terminal Type	Location	Number
Smart, Synchronous	HO	20
	HO - Maint	3
Smart, Asynchronous	HO	5
	R - Maint	4
	R - O5	4
	R - O4	4
	R - O3	4
	R - O2	4
	R - O1	6
Dumb, CRT	HO	8
	HO - MAINT	1
	R - MAINT	3
	R - O5	4
	R - O4	2
	R - O3	0
	R - O2	0
	R - O1	0
Dumb, Hardcopy	HO	2
	HO - MAINT	1
	R - MAINT	3
	R - O5	2
	R - O4	2
	R - O3	2
	R - O2	4
	R - O1	34

HO   = Home office
HO - MAINT   = Home Office Maintenance
R - MAINT   = Remote Maintenance (2)
R - On   = Remote freight office with n terminals

home office maintenance shop has three smart synchronous terminals, one dumb asynchronous CRT, and one hard copy terminal. Each of the other two maintenance shops has two smart asynchronous terminals and three dumb terminals. Of the dumb terminals, one shop has two hard copy terminals and one CRT, while the other has two CRTs and one hard copy terminal.

Of the 50 remote freight offices, 34 have only one terminal, a dumb hard copy device. Six other single terminal offices have smart asynchronous terminals with attached printers. Ten remote offices have more than one terminal. Two have five terminals, two have four, two have three, and four have two. All ten multiple terminal offices have a hard copy terminal and a smart asynchronous terminal. A few of these offices also have a dumb asynchronous CRT. Most locations operate at transmission speeds of 1200 bits per second. A few of the large offices transmit data at 2400 bits per second. The speed depends on the modems available at that site.

Each remote office would like to expand its computer use. They have expressed a need for word processing, database, and scheduling applications. Most of the offices also are interested in applications such as spreadsheet. Remote offices would use the computer facilities more if availability were better. The hard copy terminals located in most of the remote offices are too slow to support a significant level of input and output. Moreover, the hard copy devices are incapable of supporting the page mode interface required by many of AFL's applications. Finally, if additional capability is provided at the remote locations, it must be accompanied by a training program.

MICROCOMPUTER-TO-HOST COMPUTER LINKS

The second section of Palmisano's report detailed the ways in which microcomputers might be linked to AFL's system. The report cited two general approaches for making these connections, local area networks (LANs) and direct host and microcomputer links. A summary of those findings follows.

Part 2. Local Area Networks

If a there is a concentration of microcomputers in a limited geographic area, the microcomputers can be connected to a LAN. The LAN can be connected to the AFL host computer in two general ways. First, the host can act as the network file server or simply as another node on the LAN. This applies only to a LAN located in the home office complex. A second alternative is to provide a gateway between a remote LAN server and the host. This can be used for LANs in remote offices.

A home office LAN will not solve any of the existing problems. There is no lack of application capability in the home office. Terminals are directly connected to the host, and operate at 9600 or 19,200 bps and there is a wide variety of available printers for output. With the cost constraints under which AFL is operating, upgrading all home office terminals to microcomputers is not warranted at this time.

In a few instances, microcomputers could be used effectively in the home office. These instances all involve CPU intensive applications, for example, graphics and scheduling, that can be effectively implemented on microcomputers. Off-loading these tasks will decrease the work load on the host. The number of home office terminals using these applications is so few and their locations so widely distributed, that little benefit will result from placing them on a LAN.

(For considerations regarding using LANs in the remote offices with multiple terminals, refer to Case 1, the Balboa Insurance Agency.)

The Need for Micro-to-Host Links

Two of AFL's problems can be resolved by placing microcomputers in remote freight offices. First, this can provide computing power at remote locations without increasing the costs of data communications. Second, microcomputers in remote offices have the potential of reducing the reliance on host processing, and hence can decrease the processing load of the host system.

Single Terminal Offices

Remote offices have two basic needs: additional computing power and access to data and programs on the host system. Both are available via terminals connected to the host. As stated earlier, supporting this solution will likely require an expensive processor upgrade. Additionally, to be effective, the offices will also need smart terminals to augment or replace the slow, hard copy devices, and they will need faster communications links to provide good response times for full screen data transfers. A full screen transferred at 9600 bps would require just over two seconds of line time. At 1200 bps the same transfer would take over sixteen seconds.

Upgrading the slow, hard copy terminals with smart video display units operating at 1200 bps is, therefore, difficult to cost justify. An alternative is to replace the hard copy terminals with microcomputers. Microcomputers and microcomputer software can meet most of the local processing needs. In AFL's case, to be effective, the software needs to be stored locally. Downloading software like word processing or spreadsheet programs at 1200 bps or even 9600 bps is very time consuming. For example, if down loading a spreadsheet program requires that 200,000 bytes of code be transferred, at 9600 bps, the transfer will take in excess of 200 seconds or over three minutes. Moreover, with this approach, data communications line utilization will increase and incur additional line costs.

Thus, to provide an effective work environment, all microcomputers installed in local offices will need hard disk drives, modems, and locally resident application software. The availability of local processing does not, however, eliminate the need to periodically connect to the host processor. Local offices have a daily need for data stored on the host, must send data to the host, and use a few host resident programs that are not readily available on the microcomputers. Therefore, a link must be established between microcomputers and the host.

Implementing Microcomputer-to-Host Links

Host to microcomputer links can be established in a variety of ways. Transmission to and from the host can use asynchronous or synchronous protocols. Under each of these protocols there are a variety of ways that a microcomputer can represent itself to a host. These ways are referred to as terminal emulation. Thus, with an asynchronous interface, a microcomputer can appear to the host as one of a variety of terminals. In synchronous mode, the microcomputer can emulate terminals like the IBM 3270. Terminal emulation is accomplished through a cooperative effort of hardware and software. Effecting these capabilities requires a transmission medium and two basic elements, hardware and software. A variety of options are available.

Hardware. The hardware necessary to connect a microcomputer to a host is a logic card that interfaces to the communications medium. The logic card occupies a microcomputer's expansion slot or is combined with other logic cards on a multi-function board (which also occupies an expansion slot).

For asynchronous communications, the required hardware is usually a serial card--a standard component of many microcomputers--and a low cost option on others (usually under $75).

Synchronous interfaces are less common and more expensive than asynchronous ones. The most common synchronous interface is an IBM 3270 terminal emulation. This is a practical interface for IBM systems and for many non-IBM systems that support the IBM 3270 protocol.

A third way in which a microcomputer can interface to a host is via a protocol converter. Usually, for micro-to-mainframe connections the protocol converter attaches to a serial port on the microcomputer; synchronous microcomputer ports can be used as well, though synchronous ports are more expensive than asynchronous ports. If synchronous transmission is required, the protocol converters usually provide asynchronous to synchronous conversion. This type of interface is thus often a variation of the asynchronous interface. On the host side of the link, the microcomputer is connected like any standard terminal.

Software. The hardware provides the physical interface to the host, but software is also necessary on both sides of the connection. If the microcomputer's only function during the connection is to run applications that can be run on a terminal, then no special software on the host end is required. That is, the host is unable to distinguish between a terminal and a microcomputer connected in this way, and the host software is standard application programs.

In terminal emulation mode, communications software needs to run at the microcomputer end of the connection. This is the terminal emulation software that makes the microcomputer look like a terminal.

When a microcomputer is used to emulate a terminal, there is usually a difference between either the microcomputer and the emulated terminal's display monitor or between their keyboards or both. It is the responsibility of the terminal emulation software to accommodate these differences. Thus, the terminal emulation software may have to accept a combination of key strokes from the microcomputer's keyboard and map those keystrokes to an equivalent set of characters that represent a key on the terminal being emulated. For example, suppose the terminal being emulated has sixteen function keys and the microcomputer has only ten. In this case, a combination of microcomputer keystrokes, for instance ALT-F6, may be needed to represent the terminal's sixteenth function key. Moreover, the emulation software must send terminal control sequences expected by the host and must react to terminal control sequences sent from the host. For example, the emulation software needs to accept cursor positioning commands from the host and to react to them appropriately.

Using a microcomputer only to emulate a dumb or smart terminal does not fully exploit the microcomputer's capabilities. Because a microcomputer has local processing and data storage capabilities, it can be used to participate more actively in a host application. One of the most common functions that transcends simple terminal emulation is data or file transfers from microcomputer to host or from host to microcomputer, called uploading and downloading respectively. Consider downloading data from a host database to a microcomputer. Such data transfers have three components, extraction, transfer, and formatting.

Extraction. Ordinarily, the entire host database is not transferred to the microcomputer. There are several reasons for this, the most significant of which is that many host databases are too large to fit on the disks of a typical microcomputer. Second, the microcomputer user often is only interested in looking at specific subsets of data in the database. For example, a marketing manager may be interested only in shipments for a particular customer during the last quarter.

Therefore, rather than sending the entire database, usually the required data are first extracted from the host database; only the extracted subset of data are transmitted to the microcomputer. This may be done by either a program on the host written just for this purpose or by a database manipulation language like SQL.

A third way of extracting data is via cooperating software resident on both the microcomputer and the host. This capability has been evolving over time to provide increasingly easy extraction. Cooperative host and microcomputer processes allow the user to perform the three functions of extraction, transfer, and formatting in one step from an easy to use interface at the microcomputer. For example, the microcomputer user can enter an SQL command on the microcomputer and have the command exported to the host where it is acted on by a database server. The data will then be returned to the microcomputer in a proper format. In contrast, extracting data using a utility on the host requires the microcomputer user to establish himself or herself as a user on the host, run the utility to create a new file to be transferred, and then use a file transfer program to move the data from host to microcomputer.

Transfer. After extracting the data, it must be moved across the communications link to the microcomputer. A variety of methods exist for doing this. Common among these are cooperating software modules like Kermit, TCP/IP, Xmodem, Ymodem, and so on. These methods require that data transfer software reside on both the host and the microcomputer and that host and microcomputer software communicate with each other.

For example, to use Kermit, the microcomputer user might enter the terminal emulation mode on the microcomputer, establish a connection with the host, and login to the host system. On the host, the microcomputer user starts the host half of the Kermit session and requests the host Kermit module to send a file across the link to the microcomputer. The microcomputer user then switches back to the microcomputer and invokes Kermit there. On the microcomputer side the instructions to Kermit are to receive the file. The host and microcomputer software then exchange operating parameters. After sending and receiving Kermit processes agree on the transfer protocol, transfer begins and continues until the file is transferred. The Kermit processes on both sides communicate with each other to effect the transfer. When the transfer is completed, the microcomputer user then re-establishes himself or herself on the host and completes other tasks or logs off the system and exits back to the microcomputer.

Another transfer method uses standard host application or utility software that can read data from or write data to the microcomputer. On the microcomputer side, communications software, transmits a disk file or captures the incoming data and stores it on the microcomputer's disk. For example, to transfer an ASCII file on the microcomputer to an edit program on the host, the microcomputer user might do the following.

. Enter terminal emulation and login to the host.

. Start the text editor process on the host.

. Initiate a text editor command to enter text from the microcomputer's keyboard.

. Exit back to the microcomputer and invoke a terminal emulation routine that reads the ASCII file from the microcomputer's disk and transfers it to the edit program.

. When the transfer is complete, the microcomputer user returns to the host's text editor program and exits from data input mode.

With this scenario, the host text edit program acts as though it is accepting characters from the microcomputer's keyboard. From the text editor's perspective, the data it received was being typed directly by the microcomputer user.

Formatting. The third data transfer step is to reformat the data to make it compatible for use on the microcomputer. This step can be accomplished on either or both sides of the connection. Examples of formatting that might need to be accomplished include:

. Changing data codes, for example, EBCDIC to ASCII.

. Changing data formats, for example, packed decimal to binary.

. Changing organization, for example, from a database record format to a comma delimited format for importing into a spreadsheet.

An important consideration in effecting a good working interface between the host and the microcomputer is to select the proper software for the job that needs to be accomplished. At AFL, a microcomputer in a remote office will need to function as a terminal, as a stand-alone microcomputer, and in a data transfer mode. Software must exist to support each function.

An additional type of software that AFL may wish to use allows one microcomputer to control another over a communications link. In the following, the controlling microcomputer is called the requester and the one being controlled is called the server. Typical characteristics of these utilities include the following:

. A server station can call the requester and make the connection.

. A requester station can call the server station and make the connection.

. A user at the requester microcomputer can view the screen of the server microcomputer.

. The requester microcomputer can control the server station; that is, entering commands on the requester microcomputer's keyboard directs the activity of the server microcomputer.

. Files can be transferred between the two microcomputers.

. Unattended remote operation can occur; that is, an operator need not be present at the requester microcomputer.

. Inputs and outputs of remote sessions can be logged at either end or both ends of the connection.

Specific examples of software that provide these capabilities are given in Figure 5-2.

Figure 5-2. Remote Control Software

Software Vendor	Software Name
Meridian Technology, Inc.	Carbon Copy Plus
Norton-Lambert, Corp.	Close-Up
Triton Technologies, Inc.	Co/Session
Dynamic Microprocessor Associates of New York	PC Anywhere
Concept Development Systems, Inc.	Line Plus Master
American Video Teleconferencing, Corp.	In-Sync
DCA/Crosstalk Communications	Remote

Part 3. The Conclusion

The problem that AFL needs to resolve is how to enhance remote computing. If microcomputers are used, AFL must decide how to connect the remote microcomputers to the host. If microcomputers are used, the items needing resolution include the following:

. Transmission protocol.

. Terminal emulation.

. Data communications facilities.

. Configurations at multi-terminal locations.

. Software.

. Cost.

. Security.

. Control.

. Training.

Several of these topics have already been addressed. Considerations for the remainder follow.

Cost. The cost of adding microcomputers must be modest to avoid straining AFL's cash position. Adding microcomputers can be done in small increments over time to spread the impact of the expense.

Security. The ability to download data to a microcomputer is accompanied by certain security risks. Among these are the ability of users to illegally copy and use corporate data. AFL is not overly concerned that its employees will misuse corporate data; however, it is an issue that cannot be ignored.

Control. There is some risk that users will not always use the microcomputers in the intended manner. For example, users may introduce games and favorite word processors. Use of personal software will create data format inconsistencies and make communication among employees more difficult. Also, users may start to create and maintain local, private databases. This can lead to an uncontrolled proliferation of data throughout the company and result in data inconsistencies.

Training. To make the microcomputer upgrade effective, a large number of employees over a wide geographic area need to be trained to use the equipment. This will add to the cost of the system. These costs include preparation of education materials, travel expenses, and the cost of lost productivity.

YOU MAKE THE DECISIONS

Having reviewed AFL's situation and needs, you can help Annette Palmisano with the last section of her report, the recommendations, by answering the following questions and completing the following exercises.

1. AFL has been designing new applications. Will replacing terminals with microcomputers affect the applications design? If so, how? If not, why?

2. Assuming AFL's computer upgrade can be limited to $500,000, is the use of microcomputers cost effective (assume each microcomputer costs $5,000). What are the parameters that will determine the cost effectiveness?

3. Do you think the introduction of microcomputers will decrease or increase the processing load on the host? Defend your answer. Research the literature to collect evidence that either supports your conclusion. Are there conditions under which adding microcomputers will:
    a) reduce host processing requirements?
    b) increase host processing requirements?
Give examples of the conditions for each or give reasons for your negative reply.

4. What are the advantages and disadvantages of upgrading the host processor vis-a-vis installing micros?

5. Suggest an implementation approach for AFL's multi-terminal remote offices. Refer to Case 1, the Balboa Insurance Agency, for suggestions. What is the most cost effective solution for AFL? What solution has the greatest versatility?

6. In the maintenance shops, terminals are ruggedized to operate in a hostile environment. Are there microcomputers that can operate in this environment? If so, describe the features and the cost of these devices. Ensure that the microcomputers can operate in both hot and cold environments as well as dusty areas.

7. How can the remote office printing needs be satisfied with micros? Be specific in your answer.

8. Research the literature and configure a microcomputer that will meet the needs of a single terminal remote office. Provide cost estimates for all necessary hardware components.

9. Determine the software required at each remote office. In your software configuration, include the microcomputer's applications, communications, data transfer, and remote control software. What is the total cost of the required software? Document the sources of your cost estimates.

10. Combine the results of exercises 8 and 9 to get the total cost for a remote office microcomputer. Look at the literature to determine if site license agreements or volume purchases can lower the overall cost. How do your costs compare to AFL's $5000 estimate? If your figure varies from AFL's by over 20%, speculate as to why AFL's estimate is different.

11. Describe how AFL can use software that will allow microcomputers at a remote location to be controlled from a microcomputer at the home office.

12. Assuming that AFL installs microcomputers at remote locations, develop a training program for the employees there. Define what must be taught and where the training will be located. Attempt to minimize travel costs for the training sessions. Assume two people must be trained for each microcomputer being installed.

13. What new security and control concerns will AFL likely experience if microcomputers are installed at remote locations? Are these concerns different if microcomputers are installed only in the home office? Explain your answer.

14. Suppose that AFL decides to install microcomputers at the home office and move the smart terminals out to remote locations. What are the cost and remote processing implications of such an implementation?

15. A few companies have abandoned the use of central computers in favor of complete decentralized systems based on microcomputer technology. Is this a

realistic option for AFL? Explain your conclusions. What factors favor this solution? Explain you answer.

16. With your solution to the problem at remote locations, will AFL need any special host communications software? If so, what is needed? If not, why?

APPENDIX A

This appendix contains data regarding prices of data communications equipment. All the information necessary to solve cost oriented case problems can be found in this appendix. However, to make the cost estimates more up to date, you are encouraged to obtain current cost figures. The prices in this appendix are general and subject to change.

Cables

4 conductor wire	$0.29 per foot
7 conductor wire	$0.39 per foot
coaxial cable	$0.90 per foot
fiber optic cable	$1.50 per foot

Computer systems

Small scale	$25,000
Small minicomputer	$62,000
Medium minicomputer	$275,000
Large minicomputer	$550,000
Medium mainframe	$1.65 million
Large mainframe	$8.3 million
Super computer	$12 million

Data switch - 8 ports

Low speed (under 50 Kbps)	$2000
High speed (500 Kbps)	$2500

Leased Line Rates

First 100 miles	$2.25 per mile (includes monthly fee)
Next 900 miles (101-1000)	$0.94 per mile
Each mile over 1000	$0.58 per mile

Local Area Networks

    Network interface cards

slow - under 1 Mbps	$200
medium - 1-4 Mbps	$300
fast - over 4 Mbps	$400

    Network software kits (includes 2 interface cards)

slow - under 1 Mbps	$800
medium - 1-4 Mbps	$1300
fast - over 4 Mbps	$1500

Dedicated LAN server	$6000
Terminal server - 8 ports	$2700
Ethernet bridge	$2800
TCP/IP gateway - with software	$4000
Token ring MAU - 8 station	$650

Microcomputer

Low capacity	$1750
Medium capacity	$3500
High capacity	$5000

Modems

300/1200 bps	$200
1200/2400 bps	$350
4800 bps	$700
9600 bps	$1000

Packet Switched Network

      Monthly connection charge $400

      Packet charge $1.50 per 1000 packets

      Packet size   128 characters

Print spoolers

      Five CPUs, 1 Printer $950

Printers

      Laser printer $1700

      Dot matrix - high speed (400 cps) $900

      Dot matrix - medium speed (300 cps) $500

      Dot matrix - low speed (180 cps) $225

Protocol converter

      Protocol converter, all types $1000

Statistical Time Division Multiplexers

      4 Port $1200

      8 Port $1500

      16 Port $2500

Sub-LAN (Data Switches)

      Switches with file transfer capability and command switching

      8 Ports $500

      16 Ports $2500

Switched Line Rates

      Local calls $0.00

      Toll calls to 500 miles

            First minute $0.25

            Additional minutes $0.15 per minute

      Toll calls over 500 miles

            First minute $0.60

            Additional minutes $0.40 per minute

Terminals

      Dumb $400

      Smart $600

      Intelligent $1200